God-Powered: Unleashing Your Inner Superhero for a Happy, Healthy, Whole, and Rich Life.

How to activate your God-given superpowers, unravel ingrained beliefs, and create a fulfilling life in 30 days without letting societal conditioning hold you back.

Dr. Tina Brinkley Potts, PhD

Tina Brinkley Potts LLC

386 Walmart Drive, Suite 7 #39, Camden, DE 19934

inquiries@tinabrinkleypotts.com

302-208-8844

All rights reserved. No part of this book may be reproduced or transmitted in any form or by any means, electronic or mechanical, including photocopying, recording or by any information storage and retrieval system, without written permission from the authors, except for the inclusion of brief quotations in a review.

The contents of this book are intended for general informational and educational purposes only. The ideas, concepts, and techniques presented in this book are based on the author's personal experiences and perspectives.

Readers are advised to consult with appropriate professionals before implementing any strategies or making decisions based on the content of this book, especially if dealing with mental health, financial, or other significant life issues. The author and the publisher do not assume responsibility for any consequences or adverse effects resulting directly or indirectly from the use of information contained in this book.

The content is not intended to substitute for professional advice, diagnosis, or treatment. Always seek the advice of your qualified mental health provider, financial advisor, or other relevant professional with any questions you may have regarding a medical condition, mental health, or your financial situation.

The author and the publisher disclaim any liability or responsibility for any loss or damage incurred by readers as a result of applying the information presented in this book. The views expressed in this book are those of the author and do not necessarily reflect the views of the publisher. The book is not intended to be a substitute for independent professional advice.

Preface

"Our deepest fear is not that we are inadequate. Our deepest fear is that we are powerful beyond measure. It is our light, not our darkness, that most frightens us." - Marianne Williamson

This quote perfectly encapsulates the essence of the journey you are about to embark upon with this book. It is a journey of discovery, transformation, and, ultimately, empowerment. The purpose of this book is to guide you through the process of unleashing your inner superhero. By doing so, you will learn to live a life that is happy, healthy, whole, and rich beyond your current imaginations.

This isn't a book about religion.

The only thing that can separate YOU from your God given powers is YOU.

Within these pages lies a carefully curated blend of personal insights, actionable strategies, and real-life testimonies aimed at activating your God-given superpowers. This book is a culmination of years of experience gained from working with individuals just like you—those who seek more from life but are uncertain how to break free from the invisible chains of societal conditioning and personal limiting beliefs.

Throughout my career as a high-performance coach and business growth strategist, I've encountered countless individuals who were on the brink of giving up on their dreams. They were tethered by the invisible ropes of what they were taught to believe about themselves and their capabilities. Andrea, for example, a brilliant entrepreneur, was paralyzed by the fear of stepping into her potential because of deep-seated beliefs instilled during her childhood. Then there was Michael, a talented athlete, who couldn't shake off the imposter syndrome, feeling like he didn't fully deserve his victories. It was these stories, and many others, that fueled my passion to write this book. My aim is not just to change mindsets but to transform lives.

Inspiration for this work came not only from the courageous individuals I've had the privilege to coach but also from a deep-seated belief in the transformative power of recognizing and harnessing one's inherent strengths. I am grateful for the immense support and encouragement received from mentors, peers, and every person who shared their journey with me. Your stories are the heartbeat of this book.

To you, the reader, thank you for choosing to invest your time and trust in my words. I recognize the leap of faith it requires to embark on this journey of self-discovery and transformation. This book is for anyone who has ever felt stifled by their circumstances, beliefs, or societal expectations. There are no prerequisites for understanding the material, other than an open heart and the willingness to challenge and change long-held beliefs.

As we navigate through each chapter, I invite you to approach the content with curiosity, openness, and a dash of courage. The steps outlined are designed to be actionable and practical, ensuring that the transformation you seek is not only attainable but sustainable.

Thank you for your purchase and the faith it signifies. It's an honor to walk this path with you. Let's turn the page together and begin the exciting journey towards unlocking your full potential. The solutions you've been searching for are within reach—happy reading, and more importantly, happy evolving.

Introduction

Are you willing to be a forensic investigator of your belief system?

In a world where conformity often reigns supreme and fitting in is deemed safer than standing out, the journey to self-discovery and empowerment can feel like an elusive quest. For too long, society has taught us to prioritize the feelings and expectations of others, urging us to mold ourselves into predetermined shapes and roles. From the confines of traditional education systems designed to churn out obedient industrial workers to the pressures of societal norms dictating our every move, the message has been clear: blend in, comply, and seek validation externally.

But what if there's another path? What if, instead of bending to the will of external forces, we dared to focus on ourselves? What if, by turning our attention inward, we discovered not only our true potential but also the key to a happier, healthier, more fulfilled existence? What if the pursuit of personal growth and fulfillment wasn't a selfish endeavor but, in fact, the most selfless act we could undertake?

This is the premise of "God-Powered: Unleashing Your Inner Superhero for a Happy, Healthy, Whole, and Rich Life." In these pages, we embark on a journey of self-discovery and empowerment, challenging the status quo and redefining the very essence of what it means to live a fulfilling life.

At the heart of this journey lies a simple yet profound truth: You are the protagonist of your own story. You possess within you a reservoir of untapped potential, waiting to be unleashed. You are not merely a product of your circumstances or the expectations of others; you are a creator, capable of shaping your reality and manifesting your deepest desires.

But before we delve into the possibilities that lie ahead, let me share with you a glimpse of the changing world around us. As societal norms continue to evolve and paradigms shift, new opportunities emerge for those bold enough to seize them. The time has come to embrace a new reality—one where authenticity reigns supreme, and individuality is celebrated.

But perhaps you're skeptical. Perhaps you've spent so long prioritizing the needs and wants of others that the idea of focusing on yourself feels foreign, even selfish. Maybe you've been taught that self-focus contradicts your religious beliefs, that it's somehow sinful or goes against the teachings you've grown up with. If so, let me assure you: You are not alone in grappling with these conflicting messages.

I, too, once found myself torn between societal expectations and my inner yearning for personal fulfillment. Raised in a community where selflessness was revered and individual aspirations often took a backseat to collective needs, I struggled to reconcile my desire for authenticity with the pressure to conform.

But here's the truth: Despite the title of this book, *"God-Powered,"* I won't be delving into religious doctrine or theology. Instead, I invite you to consider a different perspective—one that transcends religious boundaries and speaks to the universal essence of human spirituality.

You see, I believe that each of us, regardless of our religious background or beliefs, possesses an innate connection to something greater than ourselves—a divine spark, if you will. Call it God, the Universe, Source Energy, or by any other name; the label matters less than the recognition of its presence within you.

It's this divine essence that fuels your potential, guiding you toward a life of purpose, abundance, and fulfillment. And while external influences may have led you to overlook or doubt this connection, I'm here to remind you that it exists, waiting to be acknowledged and cultivated.

But unlocking this potential requires one thing above all else: inward focus. By turning your attention inward, you begin to tap into the wellspring of wisdom and power that lies dormant within you. It's a journey of self-discovery, yes, but also one of self-empowerment—a journey that begins with acknowledging your inherent worthiness and embracing the unique gifts you bring to the world.

So, if you find yourself hesitating, unsure of whether to embark on this journey of self-discovery, I encourage you to set aside any preconceived notions or doubts. Instead, open your heart and mind to the possibility that you are far more powerful and capable than you've ever imagined. Together, we'll explore what it means to be "God-Powered," not as a religious concept, but as a recognition of your inherent divinity and the limitless potential that resides within you.

Now, let me take you back to a pivotal moment in my own journey—a moment that would forever alter the course of my life and set me on a path of transformation and empowerment.

In my own journey, I traversed this path, albeit with trepidation and uncertainty at first. In my thirties, I found myself living what appeared to be the epitome of the American Dream: a loving family, a successful career as a controller, and the trappings of material success. Yet, beneath the surface, my reality was far from idyllic. My marriage crumbled under the weight of infidelity, abuse, and shattered illusions.

For years, I clung to the belief that I was destined to endure this fate, that the confines of my circumstances defined the limits of my existence. But deep within me, a quiet voice persisted—a call to something greater, something beyond the confines of my perceived limitations.

It was a call I initially resisted, hesitant to venture into the unknown and uncertain terrain that lay beyond the confines of my comfort zone. Yet, as the tumult of my life reached its crescendo, I made a decision—a decision to heed the call, to embark on a journey of self-discovery and empowerment.

And so, I crossed the threshold, leaving behind the familiar shores of complacency and embarking on a voyage into the uncharted waters of possibility. Along the way, I encountered trials and tribulations, faced my innermost fears, and confronted the shadows that had long haunted me.

But with each obstacle overcome, I discovered within myself a reservoir of strength and resilience I never knew existed. Guided by an inner compass, I navigated the twists and turns of my journey, trusting in the wisdom that resided within me.

And then, as if by magic, the universe responded in kind. Opportunities began to present themselves, seemingly out of thin air. Clients from around the world sought my expertise, including a few notable celebrities. I found myself ascending the ranks of success, even securing a role as a co-executive producer on a major television network and streaming platform—a position I didn't even know I wanted.

These achievements were not merely strokes of luck or happenstance; they were manifestations of the power that lies dormant within each of us—the power to create, to transform, and to manifest our deepest desires.

But perhaps the most profound revelation of all was this: The greatest treasures lie not in the external accolades or material wealth but in the journey itself—in the moments of self-discovery, growth, and self-realization that shape us into the heroes of our own stories.

This book is a roadmap—a guide to navigating the complexities of modern life and uncovering the limitless possibilities that lie within. It is an invitation to embark on a journey of self-discovery, to embrace your uniqueness, and to harness the power that resides within you. That means it might be necessary for you to drop the good girl routine. (Don't take offense, I was good at it.) I lived my life wanting to be good to everyone. I wanted all to be good around me. So much so that I would believe their version. But I learned, their version might not be good for ME.

So, are you ready to awaken the superhero within? Are you ready to embrace a new reality—one where happiness, health, wholeness, and wealth are not just lofty ideals but tangible realities within your grasp? If so, then join me as we embark on this transformative journey together.

Together, we will:

- Clearing Up Your Mental Clutter

- The Power of Thought Pivoting

- Navigating Modern Distractions

- Words and Blessings

- Embracing Authencity and Truth

- Gratitude and Appreciation

- Mindful Language Use For Abundance

- Trusting Inner Wisdom

- Resilience and Prosperity After Loss

- Releasing Envy and Resentment for Prosperity

This is going to be a deep journey of self exploration. I have a companion 30 Day Prosperity Challenge. Each day you can listen to the audio and reflect on the message to reveal what could be blocking you.

https://www.happyhealthywholerich.com/pl/102590

Chapter 1: Clearing Up Your Mental Clutter

"It's time to clean house. Your mental house. If someone came through your front door with mud on their feet, would you let it stay there?"

The mid-morning sun cast its rays through the open window, stirring the aroma of freshly brewed coffee throughout the kitchen. Michael sat at the table, the newspaper lay untouched as he fixated on a gentle whirl of steam rising from his cup. The mundane tranquility belied the tempestuous thoughts itching beneath his scalp - thoughts of his faltering business, of the mortgage due next week, of how his confidence seemed to unravel thread by thread each day.

As he sipped the coffee, his subconscious replayed the criticisms from the previous day's meeting - "unreliable," "unprepared," someone had said. The words clung to him like burrs. Were they merely objective observations or seeds of self-doubt planted long ago? With each mental replay, they weighed heavier.

The sound of leaves rustling in the soft breeze and the distant laughter of children playing provided a stark contrast to Michael's inner turmoil. The weight of negative beliefs often felt insurmountable, like a torrential downpour against the flimsy umbrella of his will. Yet, he had begun to learn that the umbrella was not as fragile as he presumed. There were techniques, methods to unfurl its ribs and strengthen its fabric.

Mindfulness had become his unexpected ally; the practice of grounding his thoughts in the present, of observing without judgment. The steam from his coffee became not a nebula of worries, but just steam - warm and ethereal. It was in such small victories over his inclination to catastrophize that Michael fostered space for positivity.

He recalled, from our sessions together, the power of positive affirmations through a poignant metaphor: "Imagine your mind like a garden, where every positive thought is a seed that, with care, will bloom into resilient flowers of self-belief." The idea resonated deeply. Within the undergrowth of his anxieties, he strived to cultivate these seeds.

By lunchtime, Michael found himself at his desk, peering at the backlog of emails. The usual trepidation was there, but so was a newfound curiosity - what opportunities might these messages hold? He adopted a simple yet tangible system: for each negative assumption, he would write down a counteracting affirmation. The physical act itself was cathartic, a declaration of defiance against the ingrained patterns of thought that had confined him.

The clock ticked ceaselessly, a reminder that time and tide waited for no man. Michael felt it too - the pressing urgency and the need for change. But he also recognized that Rome wasn't built in a day. It was in the gradual, almost imperceptible steps that grand distances were covered.

A knock at the door pulled him momentarily out of his reverie. His wife entered, bearing a sandwich and an easy smile. She didn't pry or prod; her presence alone was a wordless encouragement. Michael was thankful for the simplicity of the interaction, for the momentary refuge it provided.

As the day wore on, moments of doubt were chased by specks of hope, like shadows dancing with the sun. There was an ebb and flow as natural as the world around him. The ultimate challenge lay in finding balance, in steering his ship through both tranquil and turbulent waters.

The evening now approached with its symphony of crickets and the hue of twilight. Michael stood on his porch, looking out at the world that was somehow the same yet felt different. Can it be that this daily ritual of wrestling and reconciling with his thoughts wasn't a battle to be won but a pilgrimage towards understanding his true potential? What evolving landscapes await within the silent opus of the human mind?

Unlock the Door to Your Mind's Potential

Every human mind is a battle ground of thoughts, both constructive and detrimental. Understanding the profound impact these thoughts have on your life is the first step toward a remarkable transformation.

Negative thoughts and beliefs are like weeds in the fertile garden of your mind, holding back the growth of your dreams and aspirations. Yet, with the right strategies, you can uproot these weeds and cultivate a space where positivity can flourish.

Adopting techniques to release limiting patterns of thought marks the beginning of your journey with God-powered insights. These patterns, often so deeply ingrained they seem like part of your very fabric, can be unwound. Through practical actions, you can set in motion a cycle of positivity and growth that transcends your previous limitations. The techniques shared are not merely theoretical; they are actionable strategies that have proven effective in transforming lives.

Creating the space for empowering thoughts to take root is akin to preparing the soil for a new harvest. Once you clear out the old, limiting debris, you will be amazed at how quickly new, positive thoughts can sprout and grow. The empty space is not a void but a promise of what is to come—an opportunity to build a robust and fulfilling mindset aligned with your God-given purpose.

Your innate superpowers, given by God, are waiting for activation. To harness them, you must first recognize and dispel the myths that society has conditioned you to believe. Freedom from these shackles will empower you to rewrite the narrative of your life, where being happy, healthy, whole, and rich is not just possible but expected.

The path to a prosperous life is not laden with insurmountable obstacles; it is navigated through the clearing of mental clutter that obscures your potential. The subsequent chapters will arm you with the tools to unravel and transform your belief systems, but it begins here—understanding your thoughts, renewing your mind, and setting the stage for the unveiling of your inner superhero.

Success stories abound of individuals who have mastered their thoughts and forged lives of abundance and fulfillment. Their journeys, while unique, share a common thread: the deliberate purge of limiting beliefs and the nurturing of a winning mindset. These anecdotes serve as a beacon, illuminating the path that lies ahead for you.

Boldly step forward into the rest of this book with the assurance that mental clarity is not just a lofty ideal, but a very practical and achievable state. Your commitment to this process is the first declaration of your power—the power to mold your reality. Let this chapter be the foundation upon which you build a life that is not just satisfactory, but spectacular in its richness and purpose.

Negative thoughts and beliefs have a profound impact on our lives, shaping our perspective, influencing our decisions, and ultimately determining our outcomes. When we allow negative thinking to take root, it can act as a barrier to our success, preventing us from reaching our full potential and living a fulfilling life. But fear not! Understanding the impact of negative thoughts and beliefs is the first step toward breaking free from their grip. It's time to take charge of your mental clutter and create space for positivity and empowerment to thrive.

Unpacking the Impact of Negative Thoughts

The impact of negative thoughts is far-reaching, affecting every aspect of our lives. Our beliefs about ourselves, others, and the world around us directly shape our experiences. When we harbor negative beliefs, we inadvertently attract negative situations and outcomes. This isn't just a matter of perception; it's a tangible reality. Negative thoughts can create a self-fulfilling prophecy, manifesting the very circumstances we seek to avoid.

Breaking the Cycle of Limiting Beliefs

So, how do we begin to break this cycle of limiting beliefs and negative thinking? It starts with recognizing the power of our thoughts and their ability to shape our lives. By acknowledging that our beliefs are not fixed truths but rather conditioned patterns, we can initiate a process of transformation. Once we understand that our thoughts are not inherently us, we open the door to change, growth, and the cultivation of a positive mindset.

Facing Down the Internal Critic

We all have an internal critic, that persistent voice that tells us we're not good enough, smart enough, or deserving enough. It's time to silence that critic by challenging the negative beliefs it perpetuates. Each time a negative thought arises, question its validity. Ask yourself: "Is this belief based on facts, or is it a fear-driven assumption? What evidence do I have to support this belief, and is there an alternative perspective?" Recognizing the fallibility of our negative thoughts is a crucial step in releasing their grip on our lives.

Clearing Mental Clutter for Empowering Thoughts

Now that we understand the impact of negative thoughts and beliefs, it's time to clear the mental clutter they create. Just as you declutter your physical space to foster a sense of peace and order, you can declutter your mind to make room for empowering thoughts. This process involves actively identifying and challenging negative beliefs, creating space for positive affirmations, and reprogramming your mindset for success and fulfillment.

###Are you ready to shed the weight of negative thinking and create space for empowering beliefs to thrive? Let's dive into techniques for releasing patterns of thinking that hold you back!

In order to create space for positive and empowering thoughts to thrive, it's crucial to first learn techniques for releasing patterns of thinking that hold you back. Our minds can become cluttered with negative beliefs and thought patterns that inhibit our growth and potential. It's time to clear out this mental clutter and make room for perspective-shifting techniques that can set you on a new and powerful trajectory.

Identify Your Limiting Beliefs

The first step in releasing negative thought patterns is to identify your limiting beliefs. What are the recurring thoughts that hold you back? It could be a belief in scarcity, self-doubt, or fear of failure. Once you've pinpointed these beliefs, you can begin the process of dismantling them.

Challenge Your Beliefs

Once you've identified your limiting beliefs, it's time to challenge them.

Ask yourself if these beliefs are based on reality or if they are simply ingrained patterns of thinking. When you challenge the validity of these beliefs, you open the door to new possibilities and perspectives.

Practice Mindfulness

Mindfulness is a powerful tool for releasing negative thought patterns. By staying present in the moment and observing your thoughts without judgment, you can begin to detach from negative patterns and create space for new, empowering thoughts to emerge.

Affirmations and Visualization

Affirmations and visualization are techniques that can help reprogram your mind and replace negative thought patterns with positive ones. By repeating positive affirmations and visualizing your desired outcomes, you can shift your mindset and create new neural pathways in the brain.

Cultivate Gratitude

Gratitude is a powerful antidote to negative thinking. By focusing on what you are grateful for, you shift your energy toward positivity and abundance. Make it a daily practice to write down or mentally acknowledge things you are grateful for, and watch as your mindset shifts.

Surround Yourself with Positivity

The company you keep and the content you consume have a direct impact on your thought patterns. Surround yourself with positive, uplifting people and expose yourself to inspirational and motivational content. This will reinforce your efforts to release negative thinking and invite positivity into your life.

Seek Professional Help if Needed

Releasing deeply ingrained negative thought patterns may require professional help. If you find that your efforts are not yielding the desired results, consider seeking the guidance of a therapist or counselor who can provide specialized techniques and support.

As you implement these techniques for releasing patterns of thinking that hold you back, you will create the mental space necessary for positive and empowering thoughts to thrive. Clearing out the mental clutter is the first step toward unleashing your inner superhero and creating a happy, healthy, whole, and rich life.

The Power of Positivity

The mind is a fertile garden where thoughts bloom into the actions that shape our lives. To witness a magnificent transformation, we must **consciously cultivate empowering thoughts** that nurture our spirit and invigorate our aspirations. The shift begins by uprooting the weeds of negativity that have long taken up precious space. With deliberate practice, you can sow the seeds of optimism and water them with consistent, positive self-talk. Remind yourself daily of your worth and potential. Affirmations are more than just words—they're the reinforcements of the superhero within you, awaiting activation for a life of abundance and joy.

Crafting an Empowering Mindset

It's one thing to understand the need for positive thoughts; it's another to integrate them into your daily life. The first step is to **practice mindfulness**: pay attention to your current thought patterns. Catch yourself when negative thoughts sneak in and consciously redirect your focus towards gratitude and optimism. Record moments of success and contentment—however small—and use them as anchors for when doubts arise. By **systematically shifting your perspective**, you pave the way for an empowering mindset to become your natural state.

Utilize the Power of Visualization

Harness the compelling force of visualization. Picture a life where you've unleashed your God-given superpowers, breaking the shackles of limiting beliefs. Envision your goals not as distant dreams, but as imminent realities. **Visualization is a robust tool** because the mind often can't distinguish between vivid imagination and actual experiences; by visualizing success, you prime yourself for taking the necessary steps to achieve it. Allow these visions to guide your daily actions and decisions, molding reality to match your mental canvas.

Setting the Stage for Success

Creating mental space for positivity also entails **setting clear, attainable goals**. Defining what success looks like for you personally, provides a concrete target for your thoughts to align with. Break down these overarching goals into daily intentions that move you forward, bit by bit. Celebrate each milestone as proof of your progress, reinforcing that **your efforts are manifesting real-world results**. This method helps maintain morale and ensures that your positive thoughts are not just fanciful wishes but precursors to action and achievement.

Building Your Emotional Toolkit

Equipping yourself with an emotional toolkit is crucial in maintaining a positive mindset. Identify activities that elevate your mood and incorporate them into your routine. Whether it's meditation, exercise, or engaging with uplifting content, **these are your tools for resilience**. They safeguard your positive mindset and amplify your capacity for joy. Whenever faced with challenges, reach for your toolkit and remind yourself that you are capable of weathering any storm with grace and poise.

Surround Yourself with Positivity

Just as important as cultivating internal positivity is the need to surround yourself with environments and individuals that **encourage and reflect your desired mindset**. Choose to engage with people who uplift you and share your optimism. Create physical and social environments that resonate with your goals and values. This alignment between your external world and internal aspirations acts as a reinforcing loop, making your positive thoughts natural and your perceptions reality.

Embrace Continuous Learning

Keep learning and growing, because intellectual stimulation is often the spark that lights the fire of inspiration. Read books, listen to podcasts, attend workshops—any avenue that exposes you to new ideas and perspectives can also unlock novel ways to **nurture positive thought patterns**. Knowledge is a tool that shapes your beliefs and guides your actions towards a meaningful and satisfying life. It feeds the inner superhero, allowing you to approach life's challenges as opportunities for growth and mastery.

Celebrating Small Victories

Embrace the habit of acknowledging and celebrating small victories. Each day presents numerous successes that often go unnoticed. By **taking the time to recognize these wins**, no matter their size, you reinforce the success narrative within your own mind. This practice not only boosts your confidence but also acts as evidence that you are moving in the right direction. It's a reminder that every positive thought and action contributes to building the life you envision.

Fostering a Spirit of Gratitude

Finally, cultivate a spirit of gratitude. Gratitude is the antidote to dissatisfaction and disillusionment. It grounds you and provides clarity even in chaos. At the start and end of each day, reflect on what you're thankful for. This doesn't only shift your focus to abundance but also **enhances your overall wellbeing**, preparing you to receive and recognize the blessings that come your way. **Gratitude turns what you have into enough,** and more. It is the ultimate expression of positivity, transforming your perspective and, with it, your life.

Now that you understand the impact of negative thoughts and beliefs on your life, have learned techniques for releasing patterns of thinking that hold you back, and know how to create space for positive and empowering thoughts to thrive, it's time to put these concepts into action. By actively challenging and changing your negative thought patterns, you're making room for new, positive beliefs to take root and flourish.

Remember, a shift in mindset is a superpower in itself.

As you move forward on this journey, keep embracing the power of your thoughts, and the immense impact they have on your life. Use the techniques you've learned to break free from limiting beliefs, and actively make space for empowering thoughts. The benefits of this transformation will be life-changing, leading to a happier, healthier, and more fulfilling life.

Keep this momentum going as you move on to the next chapters. There are exciting benefits waiting for you, and each one will bring you closer to unleashing your inner superhero.

Chapter 2: The Power of Thought Pivoting

"The solution is as BIG as the problem. Let's change your focus."

The mid-morning sun cast a hopeful light inside the cozy kitchen where Michael stood, a half-eaten toast in hand, crumbs falling like withered leaves onto the plate below. Across from him, his daughter, Lily, chattered about her school play, but Michael's mind was elsewhere, grappling with the rough edges of a thought that persistently sought his attention.

Michael had always prided himself on his resilience, but the loss of his job had hit him harder than he cared to admit. The severance of his daily routine had left him feeling adrift in an ocean of uncertainty. He realized that he needed more than just a new job; he needed a new way of thinking. A gust of wind outside swept through the branches, rattling against the window like a reminder to shift his internal scenery.

His mind wandered to one of our text coaching sessions about reframing thoughts, and for a moment, he considered how altering his perspective could act as a catalyst for personal growth. The truth was, he missed the comfort of familiarity, but somewhere inside, he knew that embracing change could lead to a life more fulfilling than any he had known.

As Lily giggled at a spilled drop of milk shaping into a silvery continent on the table, Michael's heart swelled with a mixture of admiration and envy. How effortlessly children adapt, finding joy in the smallest transformations. He pondered on the necessity of a childlike mindset, where every obstacle is a puzzle to solve, every setback a lesson to learn.

An energetic sparrow landed on the windowsill, pecking at the glass as if to taunt Michael with its freedom. The bird's tiny wings, fluttering with purpose and ease, made Michael consider how his own mental wings had been clipped by doubt. "What if," he mused silently, "I can pivot my thoughts as easily as this bird changes direction? What if the secret to my well-being lies in my ability to shift my focus from loss to opportunity?"

As he shed crumbs onto a burgeoning pile, the act seemed to mirror how he might shed limiting beliefs. Michael's gaze then returned to Lily, who had now created a small island of spilled cereal, giggled, and declared it a new land to explore.

"Why not?" he whispered, more to himself than to his audience of one. "Why not chart a new territory within my own thoughts, where setbacks are islands, and challenges are adventures?" The room resonated with the energetic cadence of possibility, and in that instant, Michael felt a subtle, yet profound shift.

But would this new approach be enough to navigate the uncharted waters ahead?

Unlock the Superhero Within: Master Your Mindset

Our minds shape our reality, and it's essential to grasp this to unleash our fullest potential. Recognizing the transformative ability of **reframing thoughts** marks the first step towards radical personal growth. In this chapter, we delve into the potent practice of **thought pivoting**—a method that, when mastered, can become your secret weapon. It's through this precise mental maneuvering that one can convert challenges into stepping stones and align with the realms of a happy, healthy, and rich life.

Understanding the role of **mindset** is akin to discovering a compass that guides us toward the life we aspire to lead. Our thoughts exert a powerful influence on our actions, and subsequently on the outcomes we manifest in our lives. This chapter will not leave you stranded in the abstract, but will instead offer **concrete strategies** to shift your mindset efficiently and effectively, fostering a fertile ground for well-being and fulfillment. Each thought holds the potential to propel you forward or to reinforce a standstill. Choosing the former paves the way for an extraordinary existence.

Practicing active thought pivoting entails a disciplined approach to mental redirection. It's not an infrequent adjustment but a continuous, dynamic process. It liberates you from the fetters of **negative thinking patterns** and enables you to create a proactive response to life's myriad situations. You'll learn how to intercept and adjust thoughts in real-time, ensuring they serve rather than inhibit your journey. By harnessing the power of this practice, each person can augment their mental agility and embrace the God-given strength that fosters their complete well-being.

To solidify this approach, we'll examine **evidence-based practices** that have transformed countless lives. Stories of triumph over adversity do more than inspire—they provide a practical blueprint for achieving similar successes in our lives. Evoking the principles of cognitive-behavioral therapy and positive psychology, you'll witness the evidence of thought pivoting as a *catalyst for transformation*. These insights aren't meant to merely inform; they are designed to be executed and to germinate results.

Framework for Victory: Setting Goals and Measuring Progress

Adopt a **results-focused** approach to maximize the impact of thought pivoting. Set clear milestones to track your progress, enabling you to see just how far you've come. Remember that even recognizing the need for a pivot marks a significant victory in the journey of self-enhancement. Milestones serve as powerful motivators, continual reminders of the target achievements that are well within your grasp.

The chapter is imbued with an **upbeat outlook**—a bright lens through which you're encouraged to view every aspect of this transformation. The practice of thought pivoting isn't just effective; it's immensely empowering. It underscores the attainability of success with unwavering determination and concerted effort. By celebrating your resilience and the triumphs you'll encounter, a positive language is not just used; it's put into illuminating action.

Relatable Wisdom: Your Trusted Guide to Mind Mastery

Lastly, the tone of guidance throughout this chapter is akin to that of a skilled educator—one who sees your potential and understands the journey you're undertaking. It's a *conversational dialogue*, one built on trust, relatability, and authority. Rest assured that the voice guiding you is one of experience and seasoned insight, speaking to you not as a distant advisor but as a **respected colleague**. The ultimate aim is to foster not just understanding but an impactful and enduring change.

In sum, thought pivoting is an essential instrument in your toolkit for life, one that empowers you to sculpt an existence of joy, fulfillment, and abundance. It roots your every action in a consciousness attuned to growth and contribution, unlocking the superhero lying dormant within. By the end of this chapter, these tools and techniques will no longer be theoretical—they will be an intrinsic part of *your* narrative, an unstoppable force propelling you toward the extraordinary life that awaits.

Recognizing the importance of reframing thoughts for personal growth

Our thoughts have a tremendous impact on our lives. They shape our beliefs, influence our decisions, and ultimately determine the course of our actions. It's crucial to recognize that our thoughts can either propel us forward or hold us back. By reframing our thoughts, we have the power to transform our lives and achieve personal growth.

So, how do we do this? First and foremost, we need to become aware of our thought patterns. **Pay attention to the narratives you tell yourself**, the beliefs you hold about yourself and the world around you. Are they empowering or limiting? Do they support your goals and aspirations, or do they hinder them? Understanding the impact of our thoughts is the first step in taking control of our lives.

Next, we must actively work on reframing negative or limiting thoughts. When we catch ourselves thinking negatively, we can interrupt that pattern by consciously replacing those thoughts with positive and empowering ones. **This isn't about ignoring reality, but rather about choosing a perspective that serves our growth**.

Additionally, surrounding ourselves with positive influences, such as uplifting books, motivational speakers, or supportive friends, can greatly aid in reshaping our thought processes. **Our environment plays a crucial role in reinforcing the mindset we want to adopt**. By immersing ourselves in positivity, we create a fertile ground for growth and transformation.

Understanding the importance of thought reframing is a pivotal step in the journey toward personal development. It's about taking control of our mindset, actively choosing the thoughts that serve us, and ultimately, shaping the course of our lives. By recognizing the power of our thoughts, we can pave the way for a fulfilling and purpose-driven existence.

Ready to dive deeper into the transformative power of mindset? Let's explore how our outlook on life shapes our reality and influences our journey toward a fulfilling existence.

When it comes to achieving a fulfilling life, there is no denying the pivotal role that mindset plays in the process. **Your mindset is the lens through which you perceive the world, shaping your beliefs, attitudes, and actions.** Understanding the power of mindset is crucial in unlocking your full potential and creating the life you desire. By harnessing the power of your thoughts, you can propel yourself towards growth, success, and fulfillment. Let's dive into the essential aspects of mindset and how it influences your journey toward a fulfilling life.

Mindset and Belief Systems:

At the core of mindset is your belief system, which comprises the deeply ingrained convictions and attitudes that shape your perception of yourself and the world around you. **These beliefs act as the foundation upon which you build your thoughts, emotions, and behaviors.** By recognizing and understanding your belief system, you gain the power to reframe negative or limiting beliefs that may be holding you back from achieving fulfillment. It's crucial to assess whether your belief system is aligned with your aspirations and the life you wish to create.

The Influence of Mindset on Behavior:

Your mindset significantly impacts your behavior and actions. **A growth mindset, characterized by resilience, adaptability, and a focus on learning, opens the door to opportunities and personal development.** On the other hand, a fixed mindset, rooted in resistance to change and fear of failure, can lead to stagnation and missed chances for growth. Understanding how your mindset influences your behaviors allows you to consciously pivot your thoughts toward a path of progress and fulfillment.

Mindset and Resilience:

Resilience is the ability to bounce back from setbacks and challenges, and **it is closely tied to your mindset.** A resilient mindset enables you to approach obstacles as opportunities for growth, learning, and redirection. Embracing resilience in your mindset equips you with the mental fortitude to persevere through adversity, navigate uncertainty, and emerge stronger. By cultivating a resilient mindset, you can navigate the twists and turns of life with grace and determination.

A Fulfilling Life and Mindset Alignment:

Aligning your mindset with the vision of a fulfilling life enables you to approach challenges with a sense of purpose, optimism, and determination. **When your thoughts are aligned with your desires and aspirations, you gain clarity, focus, and the drive to take intentional actions toward creating the life you envision.** By consciously pivoting your mindset toward positivity, empowerment, and growth, you set yourself on a trajectory to realize your full potential and lead a fulfilling life.

Mindset and Self-Image:

Your self-image is deeply intertwined with your mindset, as it shapes your perceptions of your capabilities, worth, and potential. A positive and empowering mindset can uplift your self-image, fostering self-confidence, self-compassion, and a sense of worthiness. **By nurturing a mindset that celebrates your strengths, acknowledges your worth, and embraces self-growth, you can foster a healthy and resilient self-image that bolsters your pursuit of a fulfilling life.**

Understanding the profound impact of mindset on the journey toward a fulfilling life empowers you to take conscious control of your thoughts, beliefs, and actions. By recognizing the potential for growth, the influence of beliefs, and the power of resilience within your mindset, you can pave the way for a life filled with purpose, joy, and fulfillment. Now, let's explore how to actively practice thought pivoting to support your well-being and harness the transformative power of your mindset.

A Strategy for Transformation

Ready to pivot your thoughts actively and support your well-being? Let's dive into **Thought Pivoting**, a mind-shift technique that can transform your reality. Picture this: Your thoughts are like a steering wheel, directing your life's journey. If you turn the wheel towards negative thoughts, your life follows suit. Now, imagine turning that wheel towards positivity, towards thoughts that empower and uplift you. This is what Thought Pivoting is about – consciously choosing the direction of your mental chatter to support your personal growth and happiness.

The First Step: Awareness

Before you can pivot your thoughts, you must first become aware of them. **Awareness** is the foundation upon which change is built. Begin by actively observing the thoughts that run through your mind. Without judgment, note whether they're negative or positive. Think of this as the initial step in a scientific experiment where you're the observer, merely collecting data on your habitual patterns of thought.

Interrupt and Redirect

Once you've developed an awareness of your thoughts, the next step is to **interrupt the negative ones** with intention. This is where you act – pause, breathe, and deliberately introduce a positive thought. For example, if you catch yourself thinking, "I'm not good enough to achieve my dreams," actively replace it with, "I am capable, and I will take one step at a time to reach success."

Confirm with Affirmation

Affirmations are powerful tools in reinforcing the new, positive direction of your thoughts. They are short, positive statements that can help to focus your mindset on the outcomes you desire. Speak these affirmations out loud, write them down, or simply repeat them in your mind with conviction. Statements like "I am worthy of a fulfilling life" or "I have the strength to overcome any challenge" are not empty words but profound truths that reshape your beliefs.

Visualize the Outcome

Visualization is an astonishing technique that magnifies the effects of Thought Pivoting. It involves **creating a mental image** of the life you want to lead, complete with the emotions and sensations of those experiences. Practice this by taking a quiet moment daily to visualize your goals as if you've already achieved them, engaging all your senses to make the experience as real as possible.

Harness the Power of Written Word

Writing actively engages the brain, making the act of thought pivoting even more potent. Start a journal, and use it to pinpoint patterns in your thoughts and document the pivots you make. By doing this, you create a tangible record of your progress and reinforce the new pathways you're forming in your mind.

Cultivate Grateful Thinking

The practice of gratitude can powerfully redirect thoughts. Each day, find moments to reflect on what you're thankful for. These moments of *gratitude* will act as natural pivots, shifting your focus from negative to positive and reminding you of the abundance that is already present in your life. This habit not only improves mood, but it rewires your brain to notice more positives throughout the day.

Commit to Consistency

Transformation through Thought Pivoting is a process – it requires **commitment and consistency**. Make the techniques we've explored a daily practice. Over time, you'll find that your default thoughts become more positive, and your reactions to challenging circumstances become more constructive. As you pivot your thoughts day by day, you're also pivoting your life into alignment with that happier, healthier, and more fulfilling existence you are working towards.

Remember, the power lies within you to steer your life towards the visions of happiness and success that are aligned with your true potential. Carry these strategies with you as tools; let them be your allies in carving out the brilliant life you are destined to live. Keep the momentum going, the excitement constant, and watch as your thought patterns transform your reality.

In mastering the power of thought pivoting, you have unlocked a key to personal growth and well-being. **Recognizing the importance of reframing thoughts for personal growth** is the foundation upon which you can build a fulfilling life. By understanding the role of mindset in achieving your desires, you have taken a vital step toward creating the life you truly want. The practice of active thought pivoting is not just a concept; it is a powerful tool to support your well-being, guiding you through life's challenges.

Remember, your thoughts have the power to shape your reality. By actively engaging in thought pivoting, you are taking control of that power. Shift your mindset from limitations to possibilities, from fear to courage, and from doubt to confidence. Each time you pivot your thoughts, you are nudging your life in the direction you desire. This is not about simply thinking positively, but about actively redirecting your thoughts in a way that serves your highest good.

Thought pivoting is a skill that takes practice. Be kind and patient with yourself as you navigate this journey. Over time, with dedicated practice and unwavering commitment, you will find that your mindset naturally aligns with the life you want to create. Embrace the power of your thoughts, and watch as your reality takes shape to reflect the positive, abundant, and fulfilling life you deserve.

Chapter 3: Navigating Modern Distractions

"If what you focus on grows, what are you growing today?"

In a quaint townhouse nestling under the vastness of an azure sky, Eleanor sat, her eyes closed, in the midst of the small garden that was her sanctum. The bustling city, with its cacophony of sirens and chatter, was inconsequential to her in this moment. She was cultivating a segmented focus on thoughts, actions, and emotions, and today, her thoughts skimmed the surface of an impending decision—whether to take the promotion that would mean more money but fewer moments like these.

Her breathing was steady, a silent metronome against the backdrop of a world that never paused. A butterfly landed on the rosebush beside her—a blaze of color against the verdant. She marveled at its serenity amidst the urban sprawl. This was intentional living, she reminded herself, conscious of each pull within her senses and of every distraction that sought to dilute her focus.

With the warmth of the late afternoon sun on her face, Eleanor practiced mindfulness, inviting societal distractions into her mental script, only to gently release them with each exhale. The aroma of jasmine filled the air, grounding her in the here and now, the sweet scent tethering her thoughts from floating away with worries of the future.

A neighbor's dog barked, pulling her from her reverie—life's reminder that the world spins on, with or without one's consent. Eyes opening, she met the gaze of an old oak tree that stood witness to her journey. Its leaves whispered stories of resilience against the winter's chill and the fierce summer heat. In its endurance, she found a mirrored strength.

The lure of aspiration and success danced in her periphery, just as the shadows began their daily waltz across the lawn. Yet, was it the title she sought, or the sense of achievement? Could the true measure of success be the courage to choose contentment over conquest?

Eleanor, with eyes wiser than before, watched the first star appear. On the brink of night's embrace, she considered her path, where each step forward was both an answer and a question. How often do we forsake the whisper of our true desires for the roar of expectation?

Cut Through the Clutter of the Digital Age

In a world saturated with endless alerts and streams of information, developing a **segmented focus** on thoughts, actions, and emotions is paramount to wielding your God-given powers. This method is not about restricting your experiences; it's about enriching them. Imagine a life where your thoughts are as clear as a bell in the silence, your actions as focused as a laser, and your emotions as controlled as a well-conducted symphony. By applying **intentional thinking**, you can align your internal compass to the values and goals that matter most.

To transform distraction into action, it's essential to consciously manage those perpetual interruptions. The key lies not in fighting the waves of digital noise, but in learning to surf them with agility and grace. This is about **choosing the signals you attend to** and dismissing the noise that disrupts your harmony. Intentional living is a deliberate choice, a bold statement of self-worth in a society that demands your attention be fragmented.

Mindfulness amidst today's societal distractions is akin to finding tranquility within a storm. Rather than withdrawing from the world, mindfulness equips you to engage with it more fully, but on *your* terms. It's about recognizing that the present moment, however cluttered, holds immense potential – a potential that's unleashed through a **calm and centered mind**. Just as a superhero discerns when to leap into action, you will learn to identify the essential amidst the chaos with crystal clarity.

Adopting a segmented approach to living is not just intuitive; it's backed by evidence-based practices that have propelled countless individuals towards success. By compartmentalizing your life into manageable sectors, you empower yourself to tackle each part with renewed vigor and unwavering focus. The result? A harmonious balance where productivity and peace coexist, where your every decision is infused with divine intentionality.

Every moment offers a choice: to succumb to distraction or to rise above it. The latter demands not just awareness but practice – disciplined, daily practice. The exercises and strategies shared in this chapter are designed to be implemented immediately, woven into the fabric of your day-to-day life until they become second nature. They are not merely guidelines but tools to craft a life bursting with focus, clarity, and spiritual alignment.

It's worth repeating: **The power to navigate modern distractions lies within you**. The anecdotes and strategies in this chapter are testimonies to the strength that resides in a disciplined mind. They will serve as both a shield and a beacon, guiding you back to your path whenever the digital world seeks to intrude upon your peace.

Remember, the true measure of success is not found in how well you eliminate distractions, but in how effectively you can move through them with purpose and resolve. With each step towards mastering your inner world, you'll find the external noise fading into insignificance. This chapter is your guide to achieving a happy, healthy, whole, and rich life amidst the very distractions that threaten to undermine it. Embrace the journey, and let your inner superhero soar.

In our fast-paced and ever-distracting world, maintaining focus can feel like an uphill battle. Our attention is constantly pulled in different directions, making it challenging to stay present and productive. However, by developing a segmented focus on thoughts, actions, and emotions, we can reclaim control over our attention and cultivate a more intentional way of living.

Developing a Segmented Focus on Thoughts

Our thoughts have a powerful impact on our emotions and actions. By consciously directing our thoughts towards positive and productive outcomes, we can influence our behavior and outlook on life. Start by monitoring your thoughts throughout the day. When negative or unproductive thoughts arise, consciously redirect them towards more constructive and empowering narratives.

Developing a Segmented Focus on Actions

Intentional living requires mindful engagement in our daily actions. Rather than letting ourselves operate on autopilot, we can take deliberate steps to actively engage in each task. Whether it's completing work assignments, practicing self-care, or engaging in hobbies, focus on being present and fully committed to the task at hand.

Developing a Segmented Focus on Emotions

Our emotional wellbeing significantly impacts our overall experience of life. Cultivating a segmented focus on emotions involves acknowledging, understanding, and regulating our feelings. By being attuned to our emotional states, we can make informed choices about how to respond in various situations, ultimately shaping our interactions and experiences.

With a segmented focus on thoughts, actions, and emotions, we can embrace a more intentional and purposeful way of living. Keep reading to discover how to consciously manage distractions and maintain intentional living.

Modern life bombards us with an endless array of distractions that threaten to pull us away from our intentionality and focus. Social media notifications, constant connectivity, and the lure of instant gratification can easily lead us astray from our goals and priorities. It's crucial to develop a conscious approach to managing these distractions, ensuring they don't derail our efforts towards intentional living.

First and foremost, it's important to recognize the impact of distractions on our lives. By acknowledging the negative influence distractions can have on our productivity and well-being, we become better equipped to address and manage them effectively. It's not just about avoiding distractions, but about actively choosing where to direct our attention.

One powerful strategy for managing distractions is to **establish clear boundaries**. This may involve setting specific times for checking emails and social media, designating certain periods for focused work, and creating physical or mental barriers to minimize interruptions. By delineating these boundaries, we empower ourselves to maintain control over our attention and energy.

Another key aspect of managing distractions is cultivating

mindfulness. When we are fully present in the moment, distractions hold less power over us. Practicing mindfulness allows us to become aware of our surroundings, thoughts, and emotions, enabling us to make intentional choices about where to direct our focus.

In addition, it's crucial to **prioritize tasks and activities** to maintain a sense of purpose and direction. By prioritizing our to-do lists, we can ensure that our time and energy are channeled towards activities that align with our goals and values, reducing the chance of getting sidetracked by less important distractions.

Moreover, optimizing our physical environment can significantly reduce the prevalence of distractions. This may involve creating a dedicated workspace that is conducive to productivity, minimizing clutter, and implementing solutions to reduce noise and visual interruptions. A well-organized environment can support our efforts to stay focused and avoid unnecessary distractions.

Importantly, **self-discipline plays a central role** in managing distractions. Building and strengthening our ability to resist immediate temptations and stay committed to our long-term goals is essential for maintaining intentional living. Practicing self-discipline helps us stay on track, even in the face of compelling distractions.

Lastly, it's essential to **constantly reassess our habits and routines** to ensure they support our overall focus and intentionality. Regularly evaluating how we spend our time and energy, and making adjustments to reduce unnecessary distractions, is critical for maintaining intentional living in the long run.

By consciously managing distractions and staying committed to our goals, we can maintain a sense of intentionality in our lives, despite the myriad of external influences vying for our attention. Through the establishment of boundaries, mindfulness, prioritization, environmental optimization, self-discipline, and regular reassessment, we can navigate the modern landscape of distractions with purpose and determination.

In a world brimming with ceaseless notifications, endless scrolling, and the clamor of a 24/7 news cycle, **practicing mindfulness** stands as a beacon of tranquility. It's a tool that empowers you to weave through the fabric of modern distractions with grace and intention. Mindfulness is not just about sitting in silence; it's an **active engagement** with the present moment, rooted in self-awareness and a heartfelt connection with your inner being. It's an invitation to anchor yourself amid the tumult of everyday life, transforming the cacophony into a symphony of focused purpose.

Anchoring the Mind in the Present

To begin this transformative practice, **start simple**. Allocate short bursts of your day to attentively observe your breath, a form of meditation that serves as an anchor to the now. This simple act forms the bedrock of mindfulness and can be called upon at any moment, providing a **sanctuary of calm**. When you find your thoughts drifting towards the torrent of emails awaiting response or the social media maze tempting your attention, remember the power of a **single focused breath**. The rise and fall of your chest can become your greatest ally in reclaiming the authority over your focus and emotions.

The Art of Single-Tasking

In a multi-tasking world, single-tasking is revolutionary. Embrace it. When engaged in any activity, give it your **wholehearted attention**. If you're eating, savor each flavor. If you're walking, notice the sensation of each step. This commitment to doing one thing at a time not only **improves productivity** but also enhances your appreciation of the task at hand. Single-tasking is an active form of mindfulness that can transform mundane actions into a practice of **deep presence and gratitude**.

Technology as a Mindful Ally

While technology is often viewed as a distraction, it can also be harnessed as a tool for mindfulness. Set boundaries around your digital consumption with specific intentions, whether it's limiting the time spent on social media or curating **a feed that inspires** rather than drains you. Use reminders on your devices to prompt short mindfulness exercises throughout the day. The key is to engage with technology in ways that **support your mental well-being**, not undermine it.

Sensory Mindfulness for Full Engagement

Mindfulness can extend beyond mental exercises; make it sensory. Pay attention to the interplay of sensations around you—notice the textures, smells, and sounds that typically fade into the background. This sensory approach is especially effective for those who find seated meditation challenging. It turns the external world into a **catalyst for**

internal awareness, reinforcing your mindfulness practice with every touch, scent, and whisper.

Embracing Mindful Interruptions

Let's redefine interruptions. Instead of viewing them as annoyances, consider each interruption as a **mindful moment**. When an unexpected call or task arises, take a brief second to breathe and center yourself before responding. This pivot reframes interruptions as opportunities to cultivate resilience and adaptability, transforming them into **unexpected gifts** of self-reflection.

Building a Mindfulness Ritual

Establish a mindfulness ritual, an essential ceremony in your daily routine. It could be a morning journaling session, a nightly gratitude practice, or a weekly nature walk. A ritual infuses your practice with **sacred significance**, reinforcing the belief that your mental space is valuable and worth protecting. It's a reinforcement of your commitment to living intentionally and a powerful antidote to the noise that vies for your attention.

Community and Connection

Lastly, mindfulness need not be a solitary endeavor. Investing time in **meaningful connections** with others can deepen your practice. Engage in mindful conversations, where you listen actively and speak authentically. Share your experiences with like-minded individuals or join a meditation group. As you build a **community of presence**, you create a supportive network that underpins your journey towards focused living in a distracted world.

In the midst of the constant barrage of modern distractions, it's essential to develop a segmented focus on thoughts, actions, and emotions. By consciously managing distractions, we maintain intentional living, and by practicing mindfulness amidst societal distractions, we empower ourselves to navigate the modern world with clarity and purpose. Embracing these strategies can profoundly impact our ability to lead fulfilling lives marked by productivity, peace, and presence.

As you move forward, remember that **your thoughts, actions, and emotions** are the foundation of your life experience. Keep them in check by deliberately focusing on one at a time, allowing your mind to tackle each domain with clarity and intention. By doing so, you cultivate a heightened awareness and control over your mental landscape, fostering a more balanced and harmonious existence.

Consciously managing distractions is paramount in a world filled with constant noise and stimuli. Implement a system where you schedule times for focused work and prioritize your attention accordingly. Set boundaries with technology, identify and mitigate your personal triggers, and practice discipline in adhering to your pre-planned tasks. This will empower you to reclaim your time and direct your energy toward your most meaningful pursuits.

Practicing mindfulness in the face of societal distractions is an ongoing discipline that can profoundly impact your overall well-being.

Utilize mindfulness techniques such as deep breathing, meditation, or body scanning to ground yourself in the present moment, regardless of external influences. This practice will strengthen your ability to discern what truly matters amidst the chaos and cultivate a deep sense of inner peace and contentment.

In the next chapter, we'll delve deeper into harnessing your unique superpowers to transcend limitations and embrace a life of abundance and fulfillment. Until then, continue to cultivate your segmented focus, consciously manage distractions, and practice mindfulness. These practices will serve as the cornerstone of your journey toward a life powered by intention, purpose, and meaning.

Chapter 4: Words and Blessings

"Speak Life always in all ways."

The air was crisp and the city awoke with a burst of energy that seemed to mirror Jonathan's own determination to start anew. Each step on the bustling streets was a cadence, an affirmation of his commitment to change the nature of his words, transforming them as architects of his fate rather than the wrecking balls they had been. The chatter around him spilled over, a cacophony of tones, but it was the internal dialogues he sought to harmonize.

At the café, the steam rising from his coffee mingled with the morning light that spilled through the window, casting a glow on the newspaper he had laid out before him. Words jumped out, reminding him something I once told him, "Your speech weaves the tapestry of your life; speak with care." As the bitter coffee touched his lips, he pondered this, sifting through memories like pages of a book, apprehending instances where careless whispers had cost him dearly.

Engagements with peers used to be marred by his acerbic tongue, a defense mechanism masking insecurities. Now, as a colleague greeted him with a cheerful "Good morning, Jonathan," he returned the gesture with a genuine smile, weaving positivity into the fabric of the encounter. That moment felt liberating, as if each word of encouragement he shared laid a brick onto the path of prosperity.

Lunchtime conversations became a practice ground. The clink of silverware and murmur of deals being made served as a backdrop to his newfound vigilance over his lexicon. "Words cast spells," he would remind himself, savoring the intention behind each sentence as much as the flavors of the meal. Compliments and optimism became his repast, nurturing not only his soul but also enriching those around him.

As the day gave in to the soft embrace of dusk, the orange hues beyond the office window whispered promises of tomorrow's potential. Jonathan sat back, contemplating the subtle shifts within him. It was more than just changing words; it was a transformation of spirit. How might such shifts in language and perspective create ripples, touching the lives of those he spoke with and perhaps even those he would never meet?

He stood by the window, the city's lights twinkling like constellations of possibility, a reflection of the stars he sought within himself—stars born from the kindling of kind words and the understanding that the blessings in one's life often germinate from the soil of our speech. What changes might unfurl from the seeds he was sowing today?

Unleash the Transformative Power of Your Voice

Words are the architects of our lives. Every syllable, every pause, every intonation carries the weight of creation, with the potential to build bridges or erect walls within our very existence. As we navigate through the chapters of our lives, it becomes abundantly clear that our spoken language is not merely a tool for communication but a force capable of shaping reality. The power vested in our words can lift us to new heights of personal prosperity and well-being, or it can anchor us in the depths of despair and defeat. Recognizing this influence is the first paramount step toward harnessing an extraordinary capacity for transformation.

In the realm of activating your *God-given superpowers*, it is imperative to acknowledge that our *language* is one of these profound abilities. Our words can either nourish our souls and those of others or act as a slow poison, inhibiting the realization of our full potential. To speak is to cast incantations over our lives, for better or worse. A blessing articulated has the momentum to catalyze growth and abundance, while a curse—though perhaps not intended as such—can stifle our flourishing. This chapter is dedicated to teaching you how to cultivate a *positive and affirming language*, one that aligns with the divine purpose and power within you.

Mindful speech is a practice—one that must be honed with the same dedication as any other aspect of physical or spiritual well-being. When we engage in conversations, whether with ourselves or others, being aware of the language used is critical. It is through this awareness that we can begin to modify the narrative of our lives, sculpting our reality with the intention and precision of a skilled artisan. Words are the medium, and our lives, the canvas.

The Path to Activating Your Superpowers

Discover and Embrace Your Desires and Strengths

The journey toward harnessing the power of your words begins with self-reflection. Dedicate time to delve into your passions and your competencies. These are the beacons that can guide you toward your inherent superpowers. Journaling is an excellent method for capturing these reflections. By externalizing your thoughts and emotions onto paper, you gain clarity and insight into your true desires and strengths.

Confront and Challenge Limiting Beliefs

Our realities are molded by our beliefs. It's not uncommon to discover upon introspection that we harbor beliefs that limit us, that keep our superpowers dormant. Identifying these beliefs is like shining a light into the dark. Write them down and stand them up against the evidence of your life experiences. Do they hold true, or are they remnants of old conditioning? It's paramount that these covert saboteurs are brought to light and disarmed.

Reframe Beliefs Into Empowering Mantras

Once limiting beliefs are identified and challenged, the next critical step is to reframe them into life-affirming statements. This cognitive restructuring is akin to spiritual alchemy—transforming a potentially destructive thought into a powerful affirmation. These new beliefs become your mantras, your spells of empowerment, to be recited with conviction.

Implement Daily Affirmations with Intent

Harnessing the power of daily affirmations is akin to programming a computer—your subconscious mind. Write down affirmations that resonate with the superpowers you aim to activate. Speak them aloud, with the unwavering conviction of someone who knows their inherent worth and potential. Visualization complements this; see yourself already in possession of the superpower you desire. Embody it in your mind, and soon you'll manifest it in your reality.

Taking Inspired Action as Your Superhero Self

As with any power, action is the key that unlocks its potential. Establish clear, actionable goals, and take consistent, inspired steps toward achieving them. Every act you take is an extension of your beliefs and the words you've chosen to live by. Remember, superpowers are designed not for mere show, but for purposeful use.

Through these steps, you will master the words of empowerment, learn how to sustain a blessing, and ward off the curses that prevent growth. By altering the language that frames our thoughts and deeds, we write a new destiny—one filled with promise, prosperity, and the unleashed power of the divine within.

Words have power. They have the ability to shape our beliefs, our actions, and ultimately, our destinies. When it comes to blessings and prosperity, the language we use carries immense weight. **Negative speech can be a formidable obstacle to experiencing the fullness of blessings and prosperity in our lives.** It's not just about the words we speak to others; it's also about the self-talk that goes on in our minds. Negative self-talk can create a barrier that prevents us from embracing the blessings and prosperity that are available to us.

How often do we catch ourselves saying things like, "I can't," "I'm not good enough," "I'll never be successful"? These seemingly harmless words are, in fact, molding our reality and hampering the flow of blessings and prosperity into our lives. Every time we engage in negative self-talk or speak pessimistically about our circumstances, we are unwittingly creating roadblocks to the blessings and prosperity that await us.

The impact of negative speech on blessings and prosperity is not a matter of mystical belief; there is evidence to support this concept. Studies have shown that individuals who consistently engage in positive self-talk and maintain an optimistic outlook tend to experience higher levels of success and overall well-being. This is not just a coincidence; it is the result of the powerful influence of positive speech on the subconscious mind and the subsequent actions and attitudes it inspires.

The first step in cultivating a life of blessings and prosperity is recognizing the impact of negative speech. **We must become aware of the language we use, both internally and externally, and its direct correlation to the experiences we attract.** By acknowledging this connection, we are empowered to reframe our language and chart a new course toward a reality filled with blessings and prosperity.

So, as we navigate through our daily interactions and internal dialogues, it's essential to remain mindful of the language we use. **Every word we speak and every thought we entertain plays a part in shaping our present and future.** Understanding this fundamental truth is the key to paving a path that is abundant in blessings and prosperity. Let's take a closer look at how we can cultivate a positive and affirming language to unlock the full potential of our blessings and prosperity.

Words have the power to shape our lives, and the language we use can greatly impact our mindset, emotions, and ultimately, our reality. Cultivating a positive and affirming language is essential for unleashing the inner superhero within us and living a happy, healthy, whole, and rich life. By choosing affirmative and powerful words, we can awaken enthusiasm and a positive attitude in ourselves and those around us.

Start by reflecting on your language: Pay close attention to the words you use on a daily basis. Are they empowering or disempowering? Are they filled with optimism or negativity? Take a moment to assess how your language may be influencing your thoughts, emotions, and interactions with others.

Replace negative language with positive affirmations: Begin the practice of substituting negative self-talk with positive affirmations. For instance, instead of saying "I can't do this," reframe it as "I am capable of overcoming any challenge." By consciously choosing your words, you can shift your mindset and open up new possibilities for growth and success.

Use the present tense: When crafting affirmations or speaking to yourself, use the present tense to reinforce the belief that what you desire is already within your grasp. Instead of saying "I will achieve my goals," say "I am achieving my goals every day." This simple shift in language can instill confidence and determination, propelling you toward your aspirations without delay.

Practice gratitude: Expressing gratitude has the power to transform your outlook and attract abundance into your life. Make it a habit to acknowledge your blessings and speak words of gratitude throughout the day. When you cultivate a habit of grateful language, you invite prosperity and positivity into your life, enriching your experiences and relationships.

Harness the power of "I am" statements: The phrase "I am" holds immense creative power, as it affirms your identity and shapes your self-perception. By consciously using "I am" statements in a positive light, you reinforce your strengths, resilience, and potential. For example, say "I am worthy of love and success" instead of dwelling on self-doubt and negativity.

Surround yourself with positive influences: Pay attention to the language used by those in your circle. Surround yourself with individuals who speak in affirming and uplifting ways, as their words can inspire and motivate you toward positive action. Choose to engage in conversations that foster growth, positivity, and encouragement rather than reinforcing limitations and negativity.

Embrace the power of visualization: Combining positive language with vivid mental imagery can exponentially enhance your ability to manifest your desired outcomes. When you verbally express your visions and dreams in a positive and affirming manner, you reinforce your commitment to making them a reality. Through the synergy of language and visualization, you create a fertile ground for your goals to materialize.

By cultivating a positive and affirming language, you uplift your spirit, foster a resilient mindset, and attract the blessings and prosperity you deserve. Your words serve as the building blocks of your reality, shaping the narrative of your life and empowering you to step into your full potential.

In the next section, we will delve into the practice of awareness of the language used in conversations and how it can further enhance our journey to living a fulfilled life.

The L.A.N.G.U.A.G.E Framework

Reflecting on Strengths and Passions

The foundation of the L.A.N.G.U.A.G.E framework begins with **L - Look Inward**. This step focuses on self-reflection, a crucial process where you delve into your thoughts, emotions, and reactions. It serves to reveal your core strengths and the issues that you are truly passionate about. As you reflect, consider past experiences, especially those moments where you've felt most fulfilled or enthused. Ask yourself, **"What strengths did I rely on in these situations? What am I deeply passionate about?"** Write these revelations down, as they will form the blueprint of your superpowers.

Assessing Innate Abilities

Moving on to **A - Assess Abilities**, this part involves a critical evaluation of the skills that come naturally to you. Each individual holds a unique set of innate abilities that, when acknowledged, can lead to great success and fulfillment. To assess these abilities, list down the tasks you excel at, those that people often turn to you for. Consider feedback you've received; what talents do your colleagues, friends, or family highlight? Assessing your innate abilities helps you to harness these talents and apply them deliberately in your everyday interactions, particularly in your language.

Nurturing Growth through Language

The next step, **G - Grow through Affirmation**, encourages the cultivation of a positive internal dialogue. Much of our external language is a reflection of our internal speech. The words you use to speak to yourself can either be empowering or debilitating. Use affirmative language to reinforce your capabilities and create an environment conducive to growth. By initiating a positive feedback loop, you are essentially telling your mind and soul, "I am capable, I am confident, I am worthy of blessings and prosperity."

Understanding Conversations' Impact

U - Understand the Impact, this stage is about comprehending the influence of your words on others. Conversations are not merely an exchange of information; they are a medium through which relationships are nurtured, and impacts are made. By becoming aware of the emotional and psychological effects your words can have, you begin to choose your language more carefully, ensuring that you imbue your conversations with intention and kindness.

Applying Affirmative Language Strategically

At the heart of our framework is **A - Apply Strategically**. This component is all about putting the insights gained from the previous steps into practice in a strategic manner. Engage in conversations with awareness, focus on delivering your message clearly and positively, and observe how different words and tones affect the dynamics. This also involves setting specific, measurable objectives for your communication, like improving team morale or increasing client trust, and using language that aligns with these goals.

Generating Prosperity through Words

G - Generate Prosperity, here the framework emphasizes the power of language to attract prosperity. The law of attraction asserts that positivity begets positivity. When you consistently speak with hope, gratitude, and anticipation of success, you begin to attract these qualities into your life. The same goes for professional settings – leaders who speak of vision and opportunity inspire teams to strive toward greatness.

Elevating Dialogues

E - Elevate Conversations, this phase is essential for taking ordinary interactions and transforming them into opportunities for connection and enlightenment. Be mindful of your word choice; aim to elevate dialogues by infusing them with meaningful, thoughtful language. Steer conversations toward subjects that can spur intellectual growth or emotional support. This not only benefits you but also those around you, creating ripples of positive influence.

Through **The L.A.N.G.U.A.G.E Framework**, you're equipped with a step-by-step process to transform your internal and external dialogues, propelling yourself towards a more fulfilling and prosperous life. Remember, language is one of the most powerful tools at your disposal, capable of both constructing and deconstructing the pillars of your life's blessings. Use this framework to imbue your words with purpose, direction, and positivity, and watch as your world transforms to match the rhetoric of your chosen narrative.

Negative speech has a significant impact on our blessings and prosperity. By allowing negative words to dominate our conversations, we inadvertently perpetuate a cycle of limitation and lack. **Recognizing the power of our words** is the first step toward harnessing the blessings and prosperity that are rightfully ours.

Cultivating a positive and affirming language is not just about uttering empty words; it's about reprogramming our beliefs and expectations. Each positive word spoken is a seed planted for a bountiful harvest in our lives. We have the ability to shape our reality through the language we use, and it's time to take charge of that power.

Practicing awareness of the language used in conversations is an ongoing commitment. It requires mindfulness and a willingness to course-correct whenever negative speech patterns seep into our interactions. The effort to monitor and adjust our language is an investment in our own well-being and prosperity.

As we move forward, let's remember that the words we speak have the power to create or destroy. Each word is a declaration, an affirmation of our beliefs and expectations. By choosing affirming, positive language, we are actively shaping a reality filled with blessings, prosperity, and fulfillment.

Chapter 5: Embracing Authenticity and Truth

"Being full of myself is a good thing."

Sunlight lazily meandered through the dusty air of the small, cluttered office where Sam sat, engrossed in the reflection that hovered on the computer screen—a far cry from the usual tedium of spreadsheets and reports. Today's struggle was personal, intangible, buried deep within and aching for release. The cursor blinked rhythmically, in sync with Sam's heart—a silent drumbeat to the tune of truth. Outside, the world hustled; cars whispered past, leaves rustled in a gentle breeze, the distant clamor of life pressing on regardless.

Within this sanctuary of solace, Sam's mind echoed with the words unspoken, heavy with the weight of authenticity yearned to be shared. Today was different, a turning point, spurred on by a conversation overheard in the hallway: "Honesty is a double-edged sword." What a simple, profound idea, presenting a challenge Sam had long avoided—embracing vulnerability by speaking one's truth.

Voices from the past danced through Sam's memories, figures of authority and affection admonishing and advising, "Guard your words, they shape your world," yet here, now, the old adage seemed a shackle to Sam's spirit. To align personal values with truthful expression felt akin to scaling a mountain, each handhold an opportunity to grasp the transformative power tucked away in the crevices of genuine connection.

Suddenly, the office door creaked open, stirring the air and drawing Sam's eyes upward. It was Pat, eyes warm, carrying the scent of the world outside, a mix of fresh earth and concrete heat. "You're quiet today, everything okay?" They asked, a simple question laced with layers of concern.

"Considering a change," Sam replied after a brief, loaded silence, encapsulating the thunderous internal debate. The conversation, neat as it was, served to punctuate the inner clamor with a real, tangible interaction that brought forth the fears, boiling to the surface.

As Pat left, promising to return with coffee, a whimsical thought struck Sam—the steam of the cup, a visible sign of the heat within. Just as it would rise from the cup, so too must honesty rise from within. Perhaps, in this moment of potential metamorphosis, empowering oneself through openness and honesty was not an insurmountable peak but an uncharted path.

As the wall clock ticked, marking the rhythm of an ordinary day, Sam considered the essence of empowerment; it was a voice rising from within, daring to be heard, to resonate with the truths of the heart. The sunset glow crept across the room, igniting the edges of a half-empty coffee cup with golden light, and Sam suspected the evening's reflection in the mirror would reveal a person braver than the morning's.

And so, the day cascaded onward with an imperative—dare to be truthful. Dare to transform. But how far will the ripples of that transformation extend? How deep can honesty root and unfurl into the lives of others?

Unmask Your Truth

Imagine standing at the edge of a chasm where on one side lies the person you present to the world, and on the other, the person you truly are; bridging this gap is the path to **authenticity and truth**. This is not about donning a cape or summoning otherworldly powers; it's about recognizing and unleashing the superpowers within you that can only be activated **when you speak your truth**. Your inner superhero thrives on your ability to be genuine and unapologetically yourself. The journey you embark on in this chapter will not only benefit your personal sense of self-worth but will also echo outwards into **every relationship and pursuit** you engage in, fostering **deep connections** and **especially profound successes**.

Authenticity is often misconstrued as a trait some people naturally have while others do not. However, it's a quality you can cultivate through thoughtful introspection and bold expression. Speaking one's truth isn't about being blunt or tactless; it's about **being honest with yourself** and others in a way that's both **compassionate and constructive**. The courage to express your thoughts and feelings can transform your life, creating a ripple effect that **enhances your wellbeing** and inspires those around you.

Empowerment takes shape when you step into the light of openness and honesty. It's easy to hide behind the facades that society constructs, but it is only when you shed these disguises that you tap into your **intrinsic power**. The alignment between personal values and truthful expression solidifies your core from which your superhero persona derives its strength. Recognizing the congruence between your inner beliefs and outer expressions allows for a life of **greater purpose** and **clarity**.

As you learn to **align your values with your words and actions**, you will find that difficult decisions become clearer and obstacles less intimidating. This alignment is a compass that directs your superhero journey, ensuring that every step you take is grounded in the truth of who you are. Moreover, **living in truth** attracts others who resonate with that same **honest energy**, building a community and environment that support your highest potential.

Begin Your Journey to Authenticity

Power and responsibility go hand in hand. As you grow into your authentic self, you are tasked with **choosing transparency over comfort, and integrity over convenience**. This chapter will provide you with actionable steps to *cultivate authenticity* in a world that often rewards conformity. You will discover how **truthful living can break the chains of societal conditioning** and liberate your **God-given superpowers**. It's about taking ownership of your narrative and realizing that you are the author of a story still being written—one where your voice is clear and uncompromising.

Equip yourself with the tools necessary to successfully navigate the complexities of life without sacrificing your truth. The **transformation that awaits you** is as significant in its depth as it is liberating in its breadth. Every facet of your existence will be touched and renewed by the authenticity you embrace: your relationships will deepen, your career will be more rewarding, and your self-esteem will be fortified. This is the chapter where you will learn to **tackle life's challenges with a genuine heart** and a **clear vision**—becoming a superhero in your own right.

Harness The Power of Your Personal Ethos

Embarking on this journey requires a commitment to personal growth and a willingness to engage in **self-reflection**. But remember, in this quest for truth, you are not alone. Drawing upon real-world success stories and personal achievements, you will gather inspiration and practical advice, grounded in evidence-based practices. Witness the power of authenticity as practiced by those who have dared to **live their truth boldly**, proving that when you are genuine, the universe conspires to assist you on your path to happiness and fulfillment.

Anticipate a thrilling adventure as you shed layers of pretense and **discover the superhero within**. Revel in the newfound strength that comes from being *genuinely you*—resilient in the face of adversity, and unwavering in your quest for a life that resonates with **joy, meaning, and authenticity**. It's time to connect the dots between your beliefs, your actions, and the extraordinary life you're capable of living. Welcome to the age of the authentic superhero—the age where your **most powerful ally is your own truth**.

Understanding the transformative power of speaking one's truth is a crucial step in unlocking our God-given superpowers. Too often, we stifle our authentic selves, fearing judgment, rejection, or failure. However, embracing authenticity and truth is not only liberating, but it also holds the key to unlocking our full potential.

By speaking our truth, we align ourselves with our core values and beliefs, creating a powerful sense of inner harmony. When we express ourselves honestly, we break free from the shackles of societal expectations and come closer to our true purpose. **Speaking our truth allows us to live with integrity and authenticity**, creating a deep sense of fulfillment and inner peace.

It's important to understand that speaking one's truth is not about confrontation or discord; it's about genuine self-expression. **By embracing our authentic voice, we communicate from a place of integrity, respect, and empathy**. This paves the way for genuine connections, enriched relationships, and remarkable personal growth.

When we suppress our truths, we create internal conflict and disharmony, leading to emotional distress and limiting our ability to tap into our God-given superpowers. On the other hand, **when we embrace our truth, we foster an environment of self-empowerment and self-respect**, paving the way for boundless personal growth and inner strength.

Through honesty and openness, we take ownership of our experiences, decisions, and emotions. **This level of accountability is an essential part of unleashing our inner superhero**, as it allows us to navigate life from a place of empowerment and self-assurance, rather than victimhood or self-doubt.

Embracing authenticity and speaking our truth is an active process – it requires unwavering determination, self-awareness, and courage. However, the rewards are immeasurable. **The transformative power of speaking one's truth is a catalyst for unlocking our God-given superpowers**, aligning us with our true purpose, and propelling us toward a life of happiness, fulfillment, and success.

Unleash the power of your authentic voice and discover a new level of personal empowerment as we delve deeper into embracing authenticity and truth.

Empowering oneself through openness and honesty begins with a deep understanding of the transformative power of speaking one's truth. It's about embracing authenticity and aligning personal values with truthful expression. By doing so, you can unlock your God-given superpowers and create a fulfilling life in alignment with your true desires and potential. This chapter explores how speaking your truth can become a catalyst for unleashing your inner superhero, empowering you to live a happy, healthy, whole, and rich life.

Understanding the Transformative Power of Speaking One's Truth

Speaking your truth has the power to liberate you from the constraints of societal conditioning and the limiting beliefs that have held you back. It's an act of courage that requires vulnerability and honesty. When you speak your truth, you signal to the universe that you are ready to live authentically. This authenticity invites positive energy and resources into your life, opening the path for your God-given superpowers to awaken and flourish.

Empowering Yourself through Openness and Honesty

Embracing openness and honesty is the key to unlocking your inner strength and resilience. When you are open about your experiences and honest with yourself and others, you become a magnet for positive change. It's a powerful act of self-empowerment, as it allows you to confront your fears, embrace your vulnerabilities, and take ownership of your story. This self-empowerment is the cornerstone of unleashing your inner superhero.

Aligning Personal Values with Truthful Expression

Living in alignment with your personal values and expressing your truth in every aspect of your life is a transformative practice. When your words, actions, and beliefs align, you create a harmonious and powerful energy that propels you toward your goals. This alignment empowers you to make decisions that are in line with your authentic self, leading to a sense of fulfillment and purpose. By aligning your personal values with truthful expression, you become a beacon of authenticity and strength, inspiring others to do the same.

Living with Authenticity: Aligning Values and Truth

Living an authentic life is about harmonizing your values with your daily expressions of truth. **Aligning personal values with truthful expression** is not just a statement of intention; it's a dynamic action you perform continuously. **Personal values** are the bedrock upon which your sense of self is built, and when your words and actions resonate with these values, you experience genuine empowerment. **Being true to yourself** in every interaction doesn't mean you'll never face dissent or disagreement. On the contrary, it often requires courage to stand firmly in your convictions, especially when they go against the grain.

Authenticity is liberating. But it also **demands consistency** between what we profess to believe and how we live. Reflect on your deepest convictions and consider whether your life currently reflects those beliefs. **Self-assessment** is a practical step towards alignment; ask yourself, are there disconnects between my values and my actions? Pinpointing such misalignments paves the way for targeted changes that honor your true self.

The Art of Honest Self-Expression

Cultivating a habit of **openness and honesty** in self-expression does more than reveal your character to others – it reaffirms and fortifies who you are. Being **authentic** doesn't imply that you're inflexible; rather, it signifies that you are willing to engage with life from a place of deep-seated integrity. **Speak your truth**, but also be willing to listen to the truths of others. This reciprocal exchange deepens mutual understanding and fosters real connection.

Many fear that truth-telling might lead to conflict or loss. However, **truthful communication** is about consonance, not just confession. It's expressing your perspectives in ways that are constructive and respectful. **Articulate your thoughts** with clarity and **commit to being understood**, not just heard. Practice active listening and empathic responses. Remember, truth spoken in love has the power to bridge divides and heal relationships.

Taking the Leap: From Values to Action

Values serve little purpose if they're stored away like ornaments, admired but untouched. **Incorporating your values** into your daily actions is a dynamic process. If you value kindness, for instance, seek out opportunities to extend compassion. Should integrity be a cornerstone of your belief system, make decisions that are transparent and fair. **Actionable values** become the landmarks by which you navigate life's complexities.

Challenging situations often compel us to **re-evaluate our principles** and the degree to which we allow them to shape our actions. It's a balance – being both flexible in approach and steadfast in values. **Transform challenges into opportunities** to demonstrate your commitment to your core beliefs. Let each decision be a testament to your dedication to live authentically.

Forging Trustworthiness Through Consistency

Consistency in aligning your actions with your values builds **trust** – trust in yourself from others, and importantly, self-trust. When you trust yourself to act according to your values, you're more likely to make choices that serve your highest interests. It doesn't mean you'll always have clear or easy choices, but it does mean you'll have a trustworthy compass — your values — guiding you.

Trustworthy individuals inspire confidence. If others see you as someone who acts with integrity, they are more inclined to trust, respect, and follow your lead. In this way, **authenticity can inspire** those around you, creating a positive impact far beyond your own immediate life.

Celebrating Progress: Acknowledging Growth in Authenticity

Living authentically is an ongoing journey — **celebrate the milestones**. Each time you voice your truth or make a choice that reflects your values, you reaffirm your identity and build strength in your convictions. **Recognize and celebrate your progress**; these moments cumulate, creating a life rich with purpose and deep satisfaction.

This is not about perfection but about progress. When missteps happen, view them as chances to learn and refine your understanding of living truthfully. **Empathy towards oneself** during these moments allows for continued growth without the shackles of undue self-criticism.

Integrating Values Into Daily Rituals

To truly integrate values into your life, **create daily rituals** that reaffirm them. This could be as simple as a morning affirmation of your intentions or as complex as a structured plan to address social injustices that conflict with your core beliefs. **Daily rituals** serve as constant reminders of who you are and the life you aspire to live, setting the stage for each day's actions to be infused with your deepest values.

Your routines can act as touchstones, bringing you back to your purpose whenever you feel adrift. By weaving your values into the **fabric of every day**, you ensure that your life is a reflection of the truest you.

Authenticity as a Catalyst for Success

Remember that authenticity has cascading effects on all aspects of life — personal, professional, and spiritual. By aligning your **inner truths** with your outward actions, you catalyze success in ways that mere conformity never could. In the workplace, authenticity can lead to **innovative ideas** and genuine leadership. In personal relationships, it fosters connections built on **real understanding** and trust. And in your spiritual journey, it enhances your connection to a higher purpose.

Living truthfully according to your values does not guarantee a life without hardship, but it does promise a life of **meaning and fulfillment**. It's an invitation to be fully present in your experiences, taking solace in the fact that you are navigating life in your own authentic way.

Living with a sense of truth and authenticity is both a commitment and a privilege. Allow your personal values to guide you and watch as the world responds in kind. Embrace the moments of alignment as affirmations of your purposeful path, and find joy in the truth that sets you free to fulfill your potential.

Embracing authenticity and truth isn't just a noble pursuit – it's a game-changer. By understanding the transformative power of speaking our truth, we empower ourselves through openness and honesty, and align our personal values with truthful expression.

Now, as we wrap up this chapter, here are a few key takeaways to keep in mind:

- **Speaking Your Truth:** Remember that speaking your truth is not about being combative or confrontational. It's about sharing your perspective, experiences, and needs with honesty and vulnerability. This is a powerful form of self-expression that can deepen your relationships and help you live a more authentic life.

- **The Power of Authenticity:** Being authentic is liberating. When you're true to yourself, you attract people and opportunities that align with your values and aspirations. Your authenticity gives others the permission to be authentic too, creating meaningful and genuine connections.

- **Alignment of Values:** Take the time to reflect on your personal values and ensure they align with the way you express yourself. When your words and actions are in harmony with your core values, you'll experience a sense of integrity and purpose that can be truly transformative.

As you move forward, continue to practice the following:

- *Self-Reflection:* Regularly take the time to reflect on your thoughts, feelings, and actions. Consider how aligned they are with your true desires and values. This will help you stay connected to your authentic self.

- *Courageous Conversations:* Don't shy away from having honest and open conversations, even if they might feel uncomfortable at first. Your willingness to engage in these conversations sets the stage for deeper connections and understanding.

- *Integrity as Your Guide:* Let your personal values be your compass. When you speak your truth from a place of integrity, you invite trust and respect into your relationships and interactions.

Remember, the more you embrace authenticity and truth, the more you'll experience the profound liberating power of being true to yourself.

Chapter 6: Gratitude and Appreciation

"No matter what, start the day giving thanks."

In a modest kitchen, where the early morning light filtered through a gauzy curtain, casting a soft glow on the hardwood floor, Elizabeth stood with her back to the humming refrigerator, cradling a cup of dark coffee. The warmth from the mug seeped into her hands, somehow invigorating and soothing all at once. Today was like any other: she had awoken to the same predictable tasks that gave structure to her days yet often went unnoticed.

As she took a sip, her eyes wandered to the little herb garden on her windowsill—basil, thyme, rosemary. They thrived here, a stark contrast to the concrete city beyond the glass. A sense of gratitude tiptoed into her heart, a soft whisper acknowledging the simple abundance of life that she overlooked in her daily rush.

Memories of her grandmother teaching her the importance of being thankful for every bit came flooding back. "When we choose to see life through a lens of abundance," her grandmother used to say, "the mundane transforms into the extraordinary." Elizabeth reflected on this as she ran her fingers over the lightly worn countertop, contemplating the history ingrained in its surface—the countless meals, the spilled secrets among friends, the laughter of family gatherings.

The clock ticked in rhythm with her thoughts—moments of scarcity had often outweighed those of plenty in her mind. She recalled days shadowed by desires for more without cherishing what was already present. It was an oversight she now longed to correct, to foster a new mindset of abundance through a conscious practice of gratitude.

As she took another sip, the sharp, bitter taste of the coffee had transformed into a sweet reminder of the often unappreciated luxury of choice and leisure. Elizabeth considered how the act of preparing a morning brew, a regularity in her daily ritual, was, in truth, a multi-sensory experience rich in its simplicity yet abundant in its ability to comfort.

Interrupted by the sound of the mail slot clinking, Elizabeth crossed the room, her reflection trailing her on the glossy floor, to retrieve a handful of envelopes. She sifted through them, noticing the everyday miracle of connection—the postman, the handwritten letters, and the miles crossed to deliver a simple message.

In this unremarkable morning, as she stood amidst the sounds of birds chirping and engines revving in the distance, Elizabeth resolved to cultivate an appreciation for the abundance in life's unadorned treasures. The shift within, she realized, had to begin with recognizing the gifts that each day brought, from the flavor of her coffee to the ability to touch and be moved by the world around her.

As she settled back into her routine with a renewed sense of purpose, one has to wonder, what are the ordinary riches of life that we can cherish today?

Unlock the Superpower of a Thankful Heart

At the core of our existence, beneath the layers of our daily hustle, lies a powerful force waiting to be harnessed—a force that is within reach but often overlooked. The act of giving thanks, a simple yet profound practice, is the key that unlocks an **abundance of joy and fulfillment** in our lives. As we delve into the dynamics of how gratitude and appreciation can dramatically transform our everyday experiences, we discover the undeniable truth that these are not just passive emotions but active states of being that can be cultivated to enrich our lives in extraordinary ways.

Gratitude has the power to shift your perspective from what's lacking to what's overflowing—turning ordinary moments into extraordinary opportunities. It's about recognizing the fullness of life and acknowledging that there's plentifulness even in what seems commonplace. By reflecting on the aspects of life we take for granted, we begin to forge a path towards a life imbued with gratefulness. It's this shift in focus that paves the way for a heart full of thanks—a heart that sees the treasure in the simple act of breathing, the beauty of a shared smile, or the warmth of the sun on your skin.

Cultivating an abundance mindset through gratitude is not just wishful thinking; it's a practical strategy backed by scientific research. Studies have shown that those who practice gratitude report *higher levels of happiness and lower levels of stress and depression*. It's a testament to the transformative power of gratitude that what we appreciate, appreciates in value. By intentionally recognizing and celebrating the good—no matter how small—we begin to expand our awareness of life's gifts and attract even more goodness into our orbit.

Appreciation, in essence, is a celebration of the riches that pervade our lives—riches that we often ignore or minimize. By fostering a genuine appreciation for the abundance in our lives, we create a vortex of positivity that echoes into every corner of our being. This isn't about blind optimism but about consciously choosing to see the wealth of blessings that surround us, even in the face of challenges and adversities. The act of appreciation is a potent reminder that our lives are filled with myriad reasons to be grateful, and it's within these reasons that we can find the strength to overcome obstacles and thrive.

To live a *thankful life* is to understand that gratitude is not an occasional act but a daily practice—one that requires conscious effort and consistent application. The truly grateful don't wait for a reason to give thanks; they give thanks and discover more reasons to celebrate life. As you embark on this journey of gratitude, remember that it starts with a deliberate choice to notice, acknowledge, and savor the goodness that exists all around you. As you do so, you'll find that your capacity for joy, health, wholeness, and wealth expands exponentially.

When you grasp the essence of gratitude, you become more adept at navigating life's ebb and flow with grace and resilience. Challenges become less daunting because you understand that there is always something to be grateful for, something that can anchor you in the present and propel you forward with hope. The practice of gratitude is not just about feeling good—it's about fostering a sense of connectedness to the divine source of all blessings, reorienting your spirit to a frequency that resonates with positivity and possibility.

Harness Gratitude, Transform Your Life

The takeaway message is unequivocal: gratitude and appreciation are more than mere sentiments. They are transformative forces that can open doors to a new world of possibilities—a world where you are the architect of your own joy. By incorporating these powerful states of being into your daily life, you become the superhero of your own story, capable of crafting a life that is not only happy and healthy but also whole and rich. Remember, gratitude is a choice, and when you choose to embrace it, you choose to access a brighter, more bountiful version of life waiting to be lived. Now, let's dive into the practical steps and real-world actions that can help you anchor this superpower into your everyday existence, ensuring that the seeds of thankfulness you plant today will bloom into the resilient, fulfilling life you aspire to lead.

Have you ever paused to reflect on the aspects of life that are often taken for granted? It's so easy to get caught up in the busyness of our daily routines, that we forget to appreciate the simple pleasures and blessings that surround us. The truth is, there is so much to be grateful for, and it's essential to take the time to recognize and acknowledge these gifts. To foster a mindset of abundance and cultivate appreciation for the richness of life, we must first reflect on what we may have been overlooking.

Here are a few areas to consider:

Family and Relationships: It's easy to overlook the love and support of family and friends when life gets hectic. Take a moment to reflect on the joy and fulfillment that these relationships bring to your life. Consider the comfort of knowing you have people who genuinely care about you and are there for you in times of need.

Health and Well-being: Often, we take our health for granted until we encounter illness or injury. Appreciating the simple ability to breathe deeply, move freely, and feel vibrant and energized is crucial for developing a sense of gratitude for the incredible gift of a healthy body and mind.

Basic Necessities: Access to clean water, nourishing food, and a safe shelter are fundamental to our existence. Yet, many people around the world are deprived of these essentials. Taking time to acknowledge and be thankful for these basic necessities helps instill a sense of gratitude and a newfound appreciation for the abundance in your life.

Opportunities and Resources: In a world filled with opportunities and resources, it's easy to overlook the privilege of an education, the freedom to pursue our passions, and access to tools and technologies that enrich our lives. Recognizing these opportunities and resources as gifts can shift your mindset from scarcity to abundance.

By reflecting on these aspects of life that are often taken for granted, we can cultivate a deeper sense of gratitude and appreciation for the abundance that surrounds us. This practice sets the stage for fostering a mindset of abundance and opening ourselves up to the richness of life.

Ready to discover how fostering a mindset of abundance through gratitude can transform your life? Read on to uncover actionable steps to cultivate a renewed sense of appreciation for the abundance in your life.

Fostering a mindset of abundance through gratitude

Gratitude is often viewed as the cornerstone of abundance. When we are grateful for what we have, we open ourselves up to receiving more. This isn't just a platitude; it's a powerful principle that can transform the way we experience life. At its core, fostering a mindset of abundance through gratitude involves shifting our focus from scarcity to plenty, from lack to fulfillment. It's about recognizing the blessings in our lives, no matter how small, and acknowledging the abundance that surrounds us.

Practice mindfulness. One of the most effective ways to foster a mindset of abundance through gratitude is to practice mindfulness. This means being fully present in the moment and paying attention to the things we often take for granted. It's about savoring the taste of a delicious meal, feeling the warmth of the sun on our skin, and appreciating the beauty of a blooming flower. By bringing our attention to these small moments, we can cultivate a deep sense of gratitude for the abundance in our lives.

Keep a gratitude journal. Another powerful way to foster a mindset of abundance is to keep a gratitude journal. Each day, set aside a few minutes to write down three things you are grateful for. They don't have to be grand or extraordinary; in fact, the simplicity of everyday blessings can be the most touching. By regularly acknowledging the things we appreciate, we train our minds to focus on abundance rather than scarcity.

Express your gratitude. Cultivating a mindset of abundance through gratitude also involves expressing our appreciation to others. Whether it's a heartfelt "thank you" to a friend, a note of gratitude to a colleague, or a loving gesture to a family member, expressing our thankfulness not only strengthens our relationships but also reinforces our own sense of abundance.

Surround yourself with positivity. The people we surround ourselves with and the content we consume greatly impact our mindset. Choose to spend time with individuals who exude positivity, seek out uplifting and inspiring materials, and avoid negativity whenever possible. Creating an environment of positivity and abundance can significantly influence our own mindset and outlook.

By fostering a mindset of abundance through gratitude, we shift our focus from what we lack to what we have. We begin to see the richness in our lives, the blessings that surround us, and the opportunities that await. When we embrace gratitude, we open ourselves up to experiencing life with joy, contentment, and an unwavering sense of abundance.

Recognizing the Wealth of the Present

Abundance surrounds us in various forms, often unnoticed as we chase future aspirations or dwell on past regrets. To truly cultivate appreciation for the bounty life offers, start by acknowledging the richness that already exists in your everyday experience. From the laughter of children to the multitude of stars at night, each moment holds treasures often overlooked. By nurturing a sense of wonder for the ordinary, you open your heart to the extraordinary splendor woven into the fabric of your day-to-day life.

Harvesting Joy from Simple Pleasures

Finding joy in simple pleasures is an actionable step to deepen your sense of gratitude. This might mean relishing the aroma of your morning coffee, or savoring the peace of a quiet walk. Pay mindful attention to these experiences, letting them fill you with ease and contentment. As you do so, you're training your mind to seek out positivity, a skill that will spill over into recognizing the abundance in other aspects of life. Each small pleasure is a building block in creating a grateful heart, capable of seeing life's wealth in its fullest form.

The Power of Saying 'Thank You'

Gratitude is not just a feeling; it is also an action. Make a habit of saying *'Thank You'*, not only to those around you but also to yourself, and to life itself. Voicing appreciation reinforces the feeling within you and signifies acknowledgment of the good you witness. The act of expressing gratitude amplifies its power, transforming internal thankfulness into an external force that can shape your interactions and relationships.

Gratitude Journaling: A Tangible Practice

Committing your thoughts of gratitude to paper can be an immensely effective strategy. Gratitude journaling anchors your awareness to abundance, documenting the good that is often fleeting in our minds. Reflect in writing on the blessings of the day, and let this practice bring clarity to the copiousness of life's gifts. As you look back on your entries, you'll realize how rich your life truly is, and this recognition can be a catalyst for continuous appreciation.

Sharing the Wealth of Appreciation

Expressing gratitude can extend beyond your personal sphere. Sharing your appreciation with others not only uplifts them but multiplies the joy you feel. Engage in random acts of kindness or offer genuine compliments. Witnessing the positive impact of your grateful spirit on others can bring a profound sense of fulfillment, affirming the limitless nature of life's abundance.

Synchronous Living: Align With Abundance

Adopt a lifestyle that aligns with acknowledgment and appreciation of abundance. This includes making choices that reflect the values of gratitude, such as opting for experiences over possessions, or prioritizing relationships and community. Synchronous living involves a conscious alignment that enhances your perception of life's abundance, encouraging a continuous cycle of gratitude and receptivity.

The Results of a Grateful Spirit

Cultivating appreciation doesn't just enhance your emotional well-being; it can lead to tangible results in all areas of life. When you live from a place of gratitude, you naturally attract more positivity, opportunities, and wealth. Be intentional in recognizing the depth of your current blessings, and let this awareness fuel your actions. You'll find that as you embrace and express thankfulness, abundance flows effortlessly towards you, enriching your world in ways once unimaginable.

By embedding these practices into your everyday life, you set the foundation for a fuller, richer, and more harmonious existence. This, in turn, positions you to tap into your God-given superpowers, propelling you towards the life you are meant to lead—a life brimming with happiness, health, wholeness, and wealth. Through gratitude, you do not just live life; you enrich it, creating an ever-expanding circle of abundance.

In cultivating gratitude and appreciation, you have laid the foundation for a mindset of abundance and contentment. By reflecting on the aspects of life often taken for granted, you have shifted your perspective to focus on the wealth of blessings surrounding you. **You have actively fostered a mindset of abundance through gratitude, recognizing the multitude of gifts and opportunities available to**

you each day.

Through cultivating appreciation for the abundance in your life, you have unlocked the power to attract even more positivity and prosperity. **By acknowledging and celebrating the abundance that already exists, you are creating a magnet for greater blessings to flow into your life.** This practice of appreciation is not just a fleeting emotional response, but a conscious decision to consciously focus on the good, thereby influencing your experiences and relationships.

Moving forward, continue to practice gratitude through daily rituals. Consistently take time to reflect on the things you are grateful for, whether big or small, and allow yourself to truly embrace those feelings of appreciation. As you do this, you are creating the space for further abundance and joy to enter your life.

In the next chapter, we will delve into the concept of "Embracing Fear and Taking Courageous Action," where we will explore the transformative power of facing your fears head-on and stepping into your full potential. Until then, continue fostering an attitude of gratitude and watch as your life becomes a testament to the abundance that surrounds you.

Chapter 7: Mindful Language Use for Abundance

"Releasing the struggle is about mind over matter."

In the lower valley of a sleeping city, where rows of brownstones stand like weathered dominoes, Emilia leans on a cold kitchen counter. The first light of dawn hesitates on the horizon, reluctant to flood her small apartment with the truth of a new day. Emilia's gaze, filled with the fog of half-formed dreams and stifled aspirations, is fixed on nothing in particular. The coffee maker gurgles like a creek swollen with spring rain, its rich aroma anchoring her to the otherwise silent morning.

She can't shake the feeling that her words—those she speaks to herself and to others—carve the path she travels. There's a hidden power in the syllables, a sort of alchemy that Emilia believes can transmute the leaden reality of her status quo into the gold of an imagined future. Her mother would murmur prayers each morning, crafting a tapestry of hope with each word, and Emilia wondered if her own words could weave her desires into existence.

A notification chimed from her phone, a message from an old friend she admired, someone who embodied abundance and seemed to draw prosperity as effortlessly as a magnet attracts iron filings. The message was an invitation to a gathering, a chance meeting of like-minded souls seeking a communal elevation of consciousness. She mulled it over, the coffee bitter on her tongue. Could these people offer her the secret language, the key to unlocking the door to her ambitions?

She stepped out the door into the brisk morning, joining the symphony of the city that slowly crescendoed around her. A man next to her at the crossing grumbled into his phone, his words heavy and dark, dripping with resentment. Emilia turned and watched a woman hushing her child with a lullaby of soft, sweet sounds. The contrast struck a chord within her; her internal narrative had danced between these two worlds, sometimes uplifted, often anchored by doubt.

As she walked, her mind danced through the lexicon of her life choices, questioning and rephrasing. Could the energy of her language reshape the opportunities and relationships she encountered? Could an intentional shift in her dialogue, a conscious selection of words rich with possibility, alter the course she was set upon?

The wind carried snippets of conversations from passersby, each a thread in the tapestry of the city's story. Emilia found herself instinctively rewriting their stories in her head, infusing them with positive affirmations, imagining their outcomes transformed by her silent interventions.

In the office, where Emilia toiled in symphony with the clicks and clacks of keyboards, she considered how each email, each casual chat by the water cooler, held the potential to build her a bridge to her goals. The whispers from her past, the visionary thoughts of the future, all now coalesced into a moment of revelation as her fingers hovered above the keys, poised to practice the conscious communication she hoped would be her metamorphosis.

Stepping into this newfound power, how might Emilia's attentiveness to her spoken and unspoken language craft a new era of personal achievement and satisfaction?

Unleashing Linguistic Alchemy: Transform Words into Wealth

Words carry the power to shape our reality, and the language we use can either limit or liberate us on our quests to lead abundant lives. This transformative chapter delves into the profound impact that mindful language use can have on our experiences and aspirations. By harnessing the potent force of words, we not only communicate with others but also with the deepest parts of ourselves, orchestrating an environment primed for prosperity and growth.

Our everyday speech often betrays the unconscious beliefs that constrain our potential. It's crucial to recognize that language is not just a tool for expression but also a mirror reflecting our inner world. Through practicing conscious communication, every conversation and internal dialogue becomes a stepping stone towards a life brimming with abundance. We can start by identifying recurring patterns in our speech and thoughts that may indicate underlying beliefs inhibiting us.

Once these patterns emerge into our awareness, the real work begins. We must dare to question them, to scrutinize their validity, and ask ourselves if they truly serve our highest purpose. This requires courage and honesty, stepping out of the familiar shadows of self-imposed limitations and into the light of introspection and change. Dissecting the origins of these patterns with open curiosity can unravel the tightly wound narratives that dictate our perceived capabilities and worth.

The adage "seeing is believing" becomes instrumental as we seek evidence to contradict and ultimately dismantle these ingrained narratives. By exposing ourselves to stories of others' achievements—those who have transcended similar beliefs—we unlock the possibility that our convictions are not absolute truths. This revelation paves the way to construct a new belief system, one fortified by empowering convictions that resonate with our highest goals and truest selves.

Next, we reinforce our restructured beliefs with **positive self-talk**. This deliberate practice shifts our focus from self-sabotage to self-empowerment. Affirmations are not mere words but are the chisel we use to sculpt our mental landscape, carving out pathways for success and well-being. Reiteration of constructive and assuring phrases leads to a profound metamorphosis of the subconscious, fostering a fertile ground for our dreams to take root.

Diving into new experiences breaks the chains of our former limitations. By throwing ourselves into situations that challenge preconceived notions about who we are and what we are capable of, we not only rebut old beliefs but also write new stories of our capabilities. This exploration is often uncomfortable, but it is within this crucible of discomfort that we truly redefine ourselves and our beliefs.

The Belief Workshop: Crafting Your Canvass of Possibilities

1. **Identify recurring patterns**: Allocate one week to self-observation. Note instances and contexts where negative patterns surface in your language, both out loud and internally. Reflect on the emotions and thoughts that accompany these moments.

2. **Question the validity of beliefs**: Over the next several days, scrutinize the beliefs influencing the patterns you have observed. *Where did these beliefs originate?* Do they help or hinder your journey to abundance?

3. **Seek evidence to challenge beliefs**: Take the following week to research and document stories or facts that counter your limiting beliefs. Surround yourself with affirming literature and conversations.

4. **Replace limiting beliefs with empowering beliefs**: Craft personalized, optimistic affirmations to negate each limiting belief you hold. Practice these affirmations daily for the next two weeks.

5. **Practice positive self-talk**: Implement a daily routine of intercepting negative self-talk and transforming it into positive affirmations. This regular exercise should continue indefinitely, becoming a natural aspect of your mindset.

6. **Embrace new experiences**: Commit to trying at least one activity outside your comfort zone each month that counters your old narratives. Reflect on your feelings and growth after each experience.

This systematic approach is designed for gradual progression and encourages consistency over a span of **two months**. The timelines are guides, not strictures. Some individuals may move faster, while others may need to extend each period to ensure a lasting transformation.

Success in this process will be evident when you notice shifts in your everyday language and thoughts, alongside an increase in positive outcomes pertaining to your aspirations. It's not merely about reaching a destination but also about evolving along your journey towards an abundant and fulfilling life. Keep track of both your linguistic adjustments and the milestones of achievement. Embrace this journey with the knowledge that your words are the architects of your destiny, building the life you desire, one syllable at a time.

Language plays a monumental role in shaping our experiences and aspirations. The words we choose to use hold the power to either uplift or diminish our spirits, to propel us towards success or keep us stagnant. As we explore the impact of language on our lives, it becomes evident that our internal dialogue and the way we communicate with others greatly influence our reality. When we become aware of this influence, we can harness the power of mindful language to manifest abundance and prosperity in our lives.

Our Internal Dialogue

The way we speak to ourselves in our minds, our internal dialogue, is a crucial factor in determining our mindset and shaping our experiences. When we continually use words of self-criticism, doubt, and limitation, we unknowingly cultivate an environment of scarcity and negativity within ourselves. Conversely, when we choose to speak to ourselves with words of encouragement, self-empowerment, and abundance, we create a fertile ground for prosperity and growth.

Communication with Others

The language we use when communicating with others also significantly impacts our experiences and aspirations. Our words have the power to either build others up or tear them down, to instill confidence or sow seeds of doubt. By practicing conscious communication, we can foster an environment of mutual support, understanding, and empowerment, ultimately contributing to the overall abundance of those around us, and ourselves.

The Power of Intentional Language

Language is not only a means of expression, but a tool for manifestation. When we use language intentionally to express our desires, goals, and aspirations, we set potent forces into motion. By articulating our aspirations clearly and confidently, we not only clarify our own intentions but also send a clear and focused message to the universe, activating the law of attraction and aligning our reality with our desires.

Understanding the profound impact of language on

our experiences and aspirations, we can begin to explore the ways in which mindfulness and intentionality can transform our lives for the better. Let's dive deeper into the power of mindful language use and discover practical strategies for cultivating abundance and prosperity through conscious communication.

Practicing conscious communication to support abundance and prosperity means being mindful of the words we use and the energy we convey. Every word we speak or write carries a vibration that can either attract or repel abundance. It's important to recognize that our language not only reflects our current state of mind but also has the power to shape our future experiences. By practicing conscious communication, we can align our words with our aspirations and create a reality filled with abundance and prosperity.

Start by being mindful of your self-talk. The way we speak to ourselves sets the tone for our experiences. Refrain from using self-deprecating language and instead, cultivate a positive inner dialogue. Affirm your worth and capabilities, and speak to yourself as you would to a treasured friend. This inner shift lays the foundation for attracting abundance into your life.

Be intentional with your spoken words. Before speaking, take a moment to consider the impact of your words. Choose language that empowers, uplifts, and inspires. By consciously selecting your words, you can create an environment of positivity and possibility, inviting abundance to flow into your experiences.

Practice gratitude in your communication. Expressing gratitude not only cultivates a sense of abundance within you but also attracts more things to be grateful for. Incorporate phrases of gratitude into your daily conversations and written communications to reinforce the abundance mindset and draw more prosperity into your life.

Use affirmations to reframe your reality. Affirmations are powerful tools for reshaping your thoughts and beliefs. Craft affirmations that reflect the abundance and prosperity you desire, and repeat them regularly with conviction. By doing so, you set the stage for these affirmations to manifest in your life.

Cultivate mindful listening. Communication is not solely about speaking; it also involves listening. Practice active and mindful listening to fully understand others' perspectives and contribute to meaningful exchanges. By being present in your interactions, you create an atmosphere of abundance where everyone feels valued and heard.

Employ the language of possibility and expansion. Instead of using limiting language that focuses on lack or scarcity, shift your vocabulary towards words of growth, opportunity, and abundance. By doing so, you foster a mindset of abundance within yourself and influence others to do the same.

Engage in positive, solution-oriented conversations. Instead of dwelling on problems, transform your conversations into opportunities to explore solutions and possibilities. By reframing challenges as opportunities for growth, you set the stage for abundance to flow into every area of your life.

The CREST Model

The journey to manifesting one's desires begins with the CREST model, a blueprint for intentional language usage and cognitive transformation. This analytical framework draws upon principles from cognitive-behavioral therapy and structures the process into five distinct phases - *Cognition, Reframing, Empowerment, Syntax,* and *Transformation*. By navigating these stages systematically, individuals can reinvigorate their internal dialogue to foster an environment where abundance can thrive.

Cognition: Awareness and Identification

The CREST model initiates with *Cognition*, where the awareness and identification of limiting beliefs take center stage. During this phase, you observe the thoughts crossing your mind and pinpoint those that may be stunting your growth. This self-awareness is foundational, giving you the insight needed to recognize patterns of negative self-talk or scarcity-focused language that could be inhibiting your path to prosperity.

Reframing: Cognitive Restructuring

Once limiting beliefs are identified, the *Reframing* stage encourages a cognitive restructuring process. Here, you challenge these beliefs by questioning their validity and searching for evidence that disproves them. Reframing is about altering your perspective, replacing negative connotations with affirmations that exude confidence and the possibility of success. This shift in perspective begins to reshape your mental landscape, making it conducive to growth and abundance.

Empowerment: Affirmations and Positive Self-Talk

Empowerment flows naturally from reframing, as it immerses you in the practice of affirmations and positive self-talk. The language you choose in this phase has power; it emboldens you to take ownership of your aspirations. By regularly articulating your capabilities and worth, you instill a belief in your ability to achieve your desired outcomes, which fuels motivation and commitment.

Syntax: Conscious Communication

At the *Syntax* stage, the emphasis is on conscious communication - not just with oneself but with the world. This involves adopting language patterns that align with your aspirations, ensuring that every word spoken or written mirrors the abundance you seek. The Syntax phase is pivotal as it translates your internal dialogue into external expressions, further solidifying your intentions.

Transformation: Manifestation and Continuous Growth

Finally, as you master *Transformation*, you harness the cumulative effect of the preceding stages. Here, manifestation is not a one-time event, but a continuous growth cycle that evolves with each reinforcing practice of the CREST model. As your language and thoughts align with your desires, you may notice opportunities and take actions that were previously obscured by limiting beliefs.

Integrating the CREST Model into Daily Life

To make the CREST model part of your daily existence, it requires rigorous practice and sustained effort. It's a dynamic tool; as you evolve, so does its application. It's about establishing new habits of mind, and this doesn't occur overnight. Regular reflection and adaptation are necessary to tailor the framework to fit your unique path and to maintain its effectiveness over time.

Incorporating the CREST model into your life means becoming mindful of every thought and word, recognizing their potential to shape your reality. Seek and surround yourself with affirming language as you engage with others, consume media, and navigate challenges. By doing so, you steadily move towards a life of abundance, powered by the very essence of creation - your words and beliefs.

Sustaining Momentum

The path to abundance isn't always linear and the CREST model accommodates for the ebbs and flows one might encounter. By monitoring your progression and recalibrating your approach when necessary, you maintain the integrity of your journey. Constantly validate the empowering effects of your new linguistic patterns through your experiences and achievements, ensuring a virtuous cycle of reflection and refinement.

By understanding and utilizing the CREST model, you facilitate a transformation in your mental and emotional realms that propels you towards the life you envision. Cultivating a mindset of prosperity through language is more than self-improvement – it's an act of creative power, where each word becomes a brick in the edifice of your dreams. Remember, the pursuit of abundance is a progressive discovery, and the CREST model serves as a guiding light along the path.

In this chapter, we've delved into the transformative power of language and its direct impact on our experiences, aspirations, and manifestations. We've learned that **the words we use shape our reality**, and that **conscious communication can support abundance and prosperity** in every aspect of our lives. Finally, we've explored the potent ability to **intentionally use language to manifest our desires**.

By recognizing the influence of language on our lives, we have opened the door to a new realm of possibilities. We have unmasked the true potential of our words and their ability to shape our reality. It is not merely about speaking positively, but about understanding the underlying power of our language to create the life we truly desire. By harnessing this power and making a conscious effort to utilize language in a mindful manner, we set ourselves on a path of abundance and prosperity.

Remember, by incorporating **positive affirmations** into our daily routine, we can reprogram our subconscious mind to align with our desires. Additionally, through **intentional manifestation techniques**, such as visualization and scripting, we can amplify our ability to manifest our dreams into reality.

So, as we move forward on this journey of unlocking our God-given superpowers, let us commit to being **intentional, deliberate, and mindful in our language use**. Let's speak with the conviction of someone who knows that each word has the power to shape their destiny. Embrace the transformative power of language and start using it as a tool to create the abundant and prosperous life you were destined to live.

Chapter 8: Trusting Inner Wisdom

"True integrity is honoring your inner voice."

It was the crisp morning air that greeted her senses first, carrying with it the musky scent of pine from the woods that bordered her rural home. Julia had awoken with a peculiar tightness in her chest, not one of illness but a gripping sensation that demanded attention. She realized it wasn't only the golden hues of the sunrise that had pulled her, half-awake, out onto the porch. It was her intuition, a silent, pulsating call that was too insistent to ignore.

In the past, Julia might have dismissed such instincts as whims; flights of fancy inappropriate for a woman of her practicality. Yet there was something about this morning, a clarity in the cool air and in the way the dew held fast to the blades of grass, that suggested her instincts held a wisdom far more profound than reason could offer. She let her gaze wander over her property – the garden she had tended so meticulously, the tire swing hanging from the ancient oak – and considered her recent restlessness.

With each step she took across the lawn, the frayed ends of her robe sweeping over the damp earth, her internal dialogue deepened. Julia recalled her mentor's words, "Trust your gut," he would say, with an enigmatic smile. She once thought it a cliché, a line borrowed from a book of less substance than those she preferred. But there, amidst the serenity of dawn, the valorizing impact of her experiences coalesced, urging her towards something yet unseen.

She paused by the garden, observing a solitary bee initiating its daily rituals. The simplicity of its existence, guided purely by nature, seemed suddenly enviable. Julia mused over how a life lead by instinct, free from the muddle of overanalysis, might unravel. Could the key to personal growth, and perhaps to the unsettled feeling that had become her constant companion, be found in such uninhibited trust?

The warmth of the rising sun brought her attention back to physical sensations – the softness of the soil beneath her feet, the gentle pull of the wind against her skin. It was as if each sense was confirming that the path to fulfillment was not to be found in external guidance, but from the internal compass we too often silence.

As she stood there, the rays of sunlight growing bolder with each passing moment, a decision began to form, unspoken yet definitive. To engage with this inner guide, whatever risk or ridicule it might invite, was now not just an option, but a necessity. A smile graced her lips as she pondered, what might she find at the end of this furtive path, illuminated not by reason's stark light, but by intuition's gentle glow?

Julia's hand instinctively reached toward the locket that hung around her neck – a keepsake containing a fragment of her grand dreams, a memento of bold aspirations not yet realized. Would her instincts guide her to their fruition? Could this be the day that she finally stepped beyond the threshold of her comfort zone, spurred by the unspoken knowledge that the time was ripe for a change? The question lingered in the air, potent and brimming with possibility: Is it not our deepest instincts that often lead us to our truest selves?

Unleash the Power of Your Instincts

In a world crowded with noise, opinions, and endless data, it's easy to overlook the **innate wisdom** that resides within each of us. The ability to **tap into your intuition** is not just esoteric folklore; it's a practical superpower that can guide you toward a more fulfilled life. This innate compass, ingrained in our being, is a guiding light towards personal growth, providing us with instinctual insights that are often sidelined by societal norms. It's time we learn how to **trust and harness these initial impulses** for a richer, more authentic existence.

The art of engaging with your inner guidance system requires a conscious choice to **turn down the volume of external influences** and amplify that soft, persistent voice within. It's recognizing that this voice—a blend of gut feelings, heart whispers, and spiritual nudges—is more than whimsy; it's a **conduit to divine intelligence** that nudges us towards our ultimate well-being. Each chapter of our lives demands decisions, and leaning into our intuition can turn those decisions from mere choices to powerful affirmations of our deepest self.

Harnessing intuition is not a passive experience; it's an **active quest for synchronicity** between your thoughts, feelings, and actions. Learning to trust your instincts is the equivalent of building a muscle – the more you **acknowledge and act upon them**, the stronger and more reliable they become. Fear and doubt often serve as the greatest adversaries to intuition, yet with decisive action, we can overcome these barriers to uncover clarity and confidence that propel us forward.

It's paramount to understand that **intuition does not dismiss reason**; rather, it complements it. This is about creating a harmonious dialogue between your rational mind and the instinctive wisdom that often holds the key to our deepest yearnings. In this chapter, we embark on a journey to explore and fortify this relationship, furnishing you with actionable strategies that place you firmly at the helm of your life's ship.

Embrace the potential within as you begin to see **intuition as a trusted confidant** in your daily life. Stories of those who have achieved remarkable success often have one common thread—**they listened to that inner voice**, sometimes against all odds. These narratives are not anomalies reserved for a gifted few; they are testament to a truth available to all. This chapter lays out the stepping stones to cultivate and elevate your inherent wisdom to make decisions that align with your most authentic self.

As your understanding of intuition deepens, you'll find that this inner guidance becomes a compass for not only big life decisions but also the seemingly trivial choices of everyday life. The cumulative effect of these choices, steered by your **inner wisdom**, shapes the trajectory of your life's journey towards one that is happier, healthier, and more harmonious.

The cultivation of this internal trust equates to empowerment, allowing you to move through the world with a **calm assurance** that your steps are guided. There is no greater peace than knowing you are the author of your own story, inscribing each chapter with the indelible ink of your soul's wisdom. Let us embark on this journey of discovery, where the destination is a life **lived in full alignment** with who you truly are.

Trusting your instincts and intuition is a vital aspect of personal growth and fulfillment. We are all born with natural inner wisdom, but often society and external influences teach us to doubt and second-guess ourselves. **Recognizing the value of intuition and instinct** is the first step in reclaiming your God-given superpowers and creating a fulfilling life. Our intuition and instincts are like a compass, guiding us in the right direction, helping us make decisions aligned with our true desires and potential.

Learning to recognize and honor your initial instincts is crucial for personal growth. When faced with a decision, our initial gut feeling often holds more truth than overthinking and analyzing. Trusting your instincts means embracing your inner wisdom and allowing it to guide your choices. This practice cultivates self-confidence and self-trust, empowering you to live authentically and confidently.

Engaging with your inner guidance enhances overall well-being and fulfillment. Intuition and instinct are not separate from logic and reason; rather, they complement each other, providing a more holistic approach to decision-making. Tuning into your inner wisdom enables you to make choices that are in alignment with your higher purpose, leading to a life of joy, success, and abundance.

Trusting your initial instincts fosters self-respect and self-empowerment. When you honor your inner wisdom, you create a deeper connection with yourself, boosting self-esteem and self-awareness. This connection strengthens your ability to navigate life's challenges with resilience and courage, ultimately leading to greater personal fulfillment and success.

By recognizing the value of intuition and instinct, you cultivate a deeper connection with yourself, elevate your decision-making abilities, and set the stage for personal growth and fulfillment. The next step is to learn how to trust your initial instincts, embrace them as powerful tools, and leverage them in your journey towards creating a fulfilling life.

Embracing your inner wisdom begins with recognizing its value. Let's explore what it means to trust our initial instincts and how to harness their power for personal growth.

Learning to trust your initial instincts is a crucial step in your personal growth journey. Our initial instincts often come from a place of inner wisdom and intuition, guiding us toward our true desires and potential. However, societal conditioning and external influences can cause doubt and hesitation, leading us to ignore or second-guess our instincts. To unleash your inner superhero and create a fulfilling life, you must learn to trust your initial instincts.

Recognize the Value of Intuition: Intuition is a powerful tool that can provide valuable insights and guidance. When you learn to tune in to your intuition, you can make better decisions, navigate challenges more effectively, and align with opportunities that resonate with your true self. Often, your initial instincts are driven by this intuition, offering a clear pathway toward personal growth and fulfillment.

Overcome Doubt and Hesitation: Trusting your initial instincts requires you to overcome doubt and hesitation. Society often emphasizes rational thinking over intuition, causing many to dismiss their initial feelings as irrational or unfounded. However, by acknowledging and embracing your instincts, you can cultivate a deeper sense of self-trust and confidence in your decision-making.

Embrace Fearless Decision-Making: Learning to trust your initial instincts means embracing fearless decision-making. It's about having the courage to follow your gut feelings, even when they go against conventional wisdom. By taking bold, decisive actions based on your instincts, you can break free from limiting beliefs and forge a path toward personal growth and fulfillment.

Cultivate Mindfulness and Self-Awareness: To trust your initial instincts, it's essential to cultivate mindfulness and self-awareness. By being present in the moment and attuned to your inner voice, you can more easily recognize and honor your instincts. This mindfulness enables you to discern between superficial fears and genuine intuitive guidance, empowering you to make decisions that align with your true desires.

Practice Self-Validation: Trusting your initial instincts involves practicing self-validation. It's about acknowledging the validity of your inner wisdom and intuition, even when others may question or challenge your choices. By validating your instincts, you affirm your worth and agency in shaping your life according to your true desires.

Seek Guidance and Support: Surrounding yourself with individuals who encourage and support your journey of trusting your initial instincts can be incredibly beneficial. Seek out mentors, friends, or community groups that foster an environment of validation and empowerment. Their guidance and support can reinforce your confidence in honoring your instincts and pursuing personal growth.

Celebrate Your Wins: As you learn to trust your initial instincts and act on them, celebrate your wins along the way. Each time you honor your intuition and make decisions aligned with your instincts, you're taking a significant step toward personal growth and fulfillment. Embrace these victories as evidence of your evolving trust in your inner wisdom, reinforcing the value of listening to your instincts.

Commit to Ongoing Growth: Trusting your initial instincts is a continuous practice. It requires commitment to ongoing growth and self-reflection. By staying open to learning from your experiences and adjusting your approach based on the insights gained, you can further strengthen your ability to trust your instincts and embrace personal growth.

Learning to trust your initial instincts is a transformative journey that empowers you to live a life aligned with your true desires and potential.

By recognizing the value of intuition, overcoming doubt and hesitation, embracing fearless decision-making, cultivating mindfulness and self-awareness, practicing self-validation, seeking guidance and support, celebrating your wins, and committing to ongoing growth, you can harness the power of your inner wisdom to create a fulfilling and purpose-driven life.

Engaging with your inner guidance is akin to nurturing a relationship with a wise mentor within you. This mentor is your intuition, an innate part of who you are, intertwined with the very fibers of your being. It is evidence of a divine connection, a God-given superpower that acts as a compass towards fulfillment and well-being. To tap into it, start by **silencing the noise** from the outside world. Carve out moments of stillness in your daily routine; whether it's through meditation, prayer, or simply a walk in nature, find that quiet space where you can hear the whispers of your soul.

Listening to Your Inner Voice

Listening attentively to your inner voice is a crucial step in making it an active participant in your decision-making process. Your intuition often speaks in subtle nudges, an inexplicable sense of knowing that doesn't shout but rather murmurs its truths. It's about paying attention to these signals — a gut feeling, a spontaneous thought, or even physical sensations that guide you towards what feels right. Trust that these instincts are aligning you with your path and purpose. *Engage with this internal dialogue*, ask questions, and be open to the answers you receive, even if they come in the form of emotions or sensations rather than words.

Honing Intuitive Skills

Like any skill, your intuitive abilities can be developed and refined. This involves intentionally practicing and reaffirming your trust in your gut feelings. When you're faced with choices, *take a moment to tune in and assess your instinctual reaction* before taking any action. Over time, you'll develop a deeper understanding of how your intuition communicates with you and how to distinguish its guidance from your fears or wishful thinking. Keep a journal of these moments and the outcomes that ensued when you followed your inner guidance; this will serve as tangible evidence of its reliability.

Scepticism vs Surrender

It's normal to encounter scepticism, both within yourself and from others, regarding the practicality of following your intuition. You might fear the risks of going against the grain or doubt the validity of your instincts. However, the path to a more empowered existence lies in the balance between rational thought and intuitive wisdom. You don't have to discard logic, but rather learn to *integrate it with your instincts.* Acknowledge your doubts, analyze them, and then return to the stillness to see what your inner wisdom has to say.

Cultivating a Trusting Mindset

Abandoning deep-seated beliefs that undermine your self-trust is a part of the process toward self-empowerment. Cultivate a trusting mindset by reinforcing the belief that you are divinely guided and that your intuition is a *direct link to that higher wisdom*. Affirmations can be a powerful tool to build this mindset. Repeat phrases such as "I trust my intuition" or "My inner wisdom guides me to my highest good" to embed these truths into your subconscious, setting the stage for a life receptive to internal guidance.

Taking Inspired Action

Once you've tuned into your intuition and received its guidance, the next step is to take inspired action. This isn't about reckless spontaneity; it's about *mindfully responding to the callings of your heart*. Whether your intuition guides you towards starting a new project, altering a relationship, or making lifestyle changes, these nudges are pushing you towards growth and fulfillment. It might require stepping out of your comfort zone, but remember, each courageous step you take reinforces the trust in your internal compass.

Recognizing Synchronicity and Affirmation

As you start acting on your intuition, you might notice an increase in moments of synchronicity — events that seem coincidental but are remarkably opportune. Embrace these as affirmations from the universe that you're on the right path. They are winks from the divine, confirming that when you trust your inner wisdom, you're supported in your journey. Appreciate and reflect on these occurrences as they are powerful reminders to keep faith in your internal guidance system.

Embracing Continuous Growth

Remember, engaging with your inner guidance is not a destination but a constant evolution. It's a lifelong journey where each experience, challenge, and decision is an opportunity to deepen your connection with your intuition. Keep an open heart and mind as you continue to navigate life's complexities. Your inner wisdom will not only lead you to fulfillment and well-being but also transform the way you experience the world, infusing every moment with a sense of purpose and richness. With patience, practice, and perseverance, you'll find that this incredible tool shapes a happier, healthier, whole, and rich life as it unveils the exceptional power you hold within.

Trusting your inner wisdom is not just a philosophical concept, it's a practical tool for navigating life with confidence and clarity. As you recognize the value of intuition and instinct, you open the door to a deeper understanding of yourself and the world around you. Learning to trust your initial instincts is not just about impulsive decision-making but about taking the time to listen to your inner voice and acknowledge its wisdom. When you engage with your inner guidance, you pave the way for fulfillment and well-being in all areas of your life.

Recognize the Value of Intuition and Instinct: Give yourself permission to acknowledge the power of your intuition. It's not a mystical force; it's a collection of your experiences, feelings, and knowledge bubbling up to provide you with insights. Embrace this as a valuable asset in your decision-making process. Take time to listen to it, respect it, and consider its input alongside other sources of information.

Trust Your Initial Instincts for Personal Growth: When you get that gut feeling or that first thought that pops into your head, don't dismiss it.

Pay attention to it and let it inform your choices. Trusting your initial instincts doesn't mean you discard rational thinking; it means you integrate your instinctual responses into your decision-making process. This can lead to personal growth, as you acknowledge and act upon the insights that come from within.

Engage with Inner Guidance for Fulfillment and Well-being: By engaging with your inner guidance, you align yourself with your true desires, needs, and aspirations. When you learn to trust this internal compass, you foster a sense of fulfillment and well-being in your life. You become more attuned to what truly matters to you, making decisions that resonate with your core values and bringing a sense of peace and harmony into your life.

As you move forward, take the time to practice these principles daily. Give yourself permission to trust your inner wisdom, and watch how it guides you towards a happier, healthier, and more fulfilling life.

Chapter 9: Resilience and Prosperity After Loss

"There is something waiting for you on the other side of loss. Are you brave enough to allow it?"

Julia's fingertips traced the sun-baked bricks of the quaint café she had frequented since yesteryear. The aroma of freshly baked pastries wafted in the air—a stark contrast to the tumult within her. The establishment buzzed with the clink of cutlery and the murmur of conversation, but to her, it reverberated with the echoes of resilience, a constant reminder of the vitality that life demands after setbacks. Her café had once been ash and dust, a casualty to an unfortunate blaze, but now, it stood stronger, its story etched in every restored corner.

An afternoon sun cast long shadows as Julia nestled in her usual spot by the window, where she would glance at the pedestrians, each absorbed in their own narrative of loss and recovery. Her own table, a once-charred relic, testified to the renewal it had witnessed, a silent companion to her musing. The resilience of the café echoed her internal conflict—a business once lost to uncertainty, now thriving, compelling her to draw parallels with her faltering career.

She remembered the disorientation, the period after being let go from a job she loved, where the future was as murky as the over-caffeinated concoctions she had been served in lesser establishments. But it was here, amid the clatter and steam, where the seeds of a new beginning had been sown. Julia dwelled on the mindset and strategies that had spirited her back then; the fortitude that revolved around the simple conviction that one closed door heralds the opening of another. She had clawed her way back with tenacity and now faced a new crossroad—a potential venture that could catapult her but brought the risk of a familiar downfall.

Obsidian eyes, dotted with hints of determination, mirrored a microcosm of bustling life outside. She realized, as she eavesdropped on the world's whispered secrets, that cultivating a mindset of abundance and wealth was not about the tangible currency that flowed through the veins of commerce but the richer currency of belief and vision within one's self. The wealth of her experiences, the richness of starting anew, was a prospective she could not put a price on, and it surged through her with the fervor of a relentless tide.

A nascent idea was taking root, tendrils entwining with her expertise and past scars, creating a meshwork strong enough to bear the fruits of her next endeavor. She focused on the palpable buzz, the energy of the café as if it transfused into her, reinforcing her resolve. The figures outside blurred into a tapestry of motion, a testament to the dance of life and its infinite pirouettes.

As Julia rose from her seat, her reflection in the window smiled back, an affirmation of the path she was about to tread. The warmth of the café lingered on her skin, and the spring in her step sang of the possibilities that tomorrow held. What if the rest of the world grasped the essence of abundance as she had in this moment, would resilience not become second nature, and prosperity but an eventuality in the stories of their lives?

From Ashes to Triumph

Every setback carves out the contours of a new beginning. In the realm of loss and disappointment, there lies a potent seed of **resilience and potential for prosperity**. It is not the occurrence of setbacks that defines our story, but rather how we bounce back and harness the treasures hidden within them. Understanding this resilience, this extraordinary capacity to recover quickly from difficulties, is your first lesson in transforming loss into a pathway toward a richer life.

Transformative **mindset and strategies** are your allies in this journey. To capitalize on them, one must delve into the mechanics of thought and action that facilitate recovery from loss. Getting up after a fall isn't just about sheer willpower; it's about learning the art of mental and emotional agility. Furthermore, cultivating a mindset of abundance and wealth beyond material riches — embracing the wealth of spirit, health, relationships, and passion — sets the stage for not only recovery but also for thriving.

Building Blocks of Resilience

Harness the power of resilience by integrating **evidence-based practices** into your daily routine. Strategies such as mindfulness, cognitive restructuring, and developing a supportive network are not merely theoretical concepts. They are real, actionable tools that have helped countless individuals emerge victorious from the grips of adversity. Your journey through loss can lead to an abundance that permeates every aspect of your being, laying a foundation for lifelong prosperity.

The Strategy of Bouncing Back

Recognize that the path to prosperity is paved with lessons learned from setbacks. Identify those lessons, and allow them to shape your vision of the future. This type of reflective practice not only strengthens resilience but also equips you with a **strategic mindset** for navigating future challenges. Assemble these insights into a personal blueprint for bouncing back, a plan that is as unique to you as your individual experiences.

Abundance in Every Breath

Cultivating a mindset of abundance involves a holistic approach. Recognize that wealth is multifaceted, encompassing emotional well-being, spiritual richness, and intellectual growth. This chapter provides **concrete steps** to embed this mindset into every facet of your life, ensuring that your definition of prosperity transcends the financial and material to include the intangible yet invaluable riches of life.

Strategic Wealth of Relationships

Your network plays a crucial role in your resilience and recovery journey. **Foster deep connections** with those around you, and learn to leverage collective wisdom and support. Each relationship in your life is a potential springboard towards greater understanding and wealth of experience. Building a community of like-minded individuals creates a reservoir of resources that can empower you through your pursuit of a full and rich life.

Cultivating Courageous Optimism

Optimism is not a passive wish for a better future; it is a **dynamic force** that propels you towards your goals. Armed with an optimistic outlook, imbued with courage and an understanding of the opportunities concealed within obstacles, you lay the groundwork for continued success. Highlighting the resilience and triumph of those who have overcome adversity motivates you to see beyond temporary setbacks and focus on the potential for greatness that lies ahead.

Action, Not Just Ambition

Merge inspiration with action and witness how the theoretical transforms into the tangible. This chapter is not merely a source of comfort but a call to **take deliberate steps** towards rebuilding and enhancing your life. By the end of this segment, you will not only be equipped with the knowledge of how to thrive after loss but also with a sequence of practical actions to start this very moment, ensuring that the prosperity you seek is not just a vision, but an inevitable reality.

Resilience is a vital skill that enables us to bounce back from challenges, grow stronger, and even prosper after setbacks. It's the key to not just surviving but thriving in the face of adversity. Understanding the power of resilience is crucial in order to harness it effectively and emerge victorious in the aftermath of loss or failure.

To weather life's storms and emerge stronger on the other side, we must first embrace the fact that setbacks and losses are inevitable. The truth is, no one is immune to misfortune. However, we can control how we respond to these challenges by adopting a resilient mindset. **Resilience involves cultivating a belief in our ability to overcome difficulties, adapt to change, and ultimately triumph despite adversity.**

It's important to recognize that resilience doesn't mean denying the pain or suffering caused by setbacks. Instead, it's about acknowledging the hardship while maintaining a forward-focused perspective. This allows us to remain solution-oriented and continue moving toward our goals, even in the face of immense difficulty. **Resilience is about harnessing the power of positive thinking to propel us forward.**

In order to build resilience, it's essential to cultivate a growth mindset. This means viewing challenges as opportunities for growth and learning, rather than insurmountable obstacles. **By adopting a growth mindset, we can reframe setbacks as valuable lessons that contribute to our personal development and overall resilience.**

Another key aspect of resilience is the ability to examine and reframe our beliefs about setbacks and failures. We must challenge any negative or limiting beliefs that may hold us back. **Instead of viewing setbacks as permanent or insurmountable, we can begin to see them as temporary and surmountable obstacles that can be overcome.**

Resilience isn't just about weathering the storm; it's also about prospering in its wake. By embracing resilience, we can emerge from setbacks with newfound strength, wisdom, and even prosperity. With the right mindset and strategies, we can not only bounce back from loss but also thrive in the face of adversity.

Ready to uncover the mindsets and strategies that will empower you to thrive after facing challenges? Keep reading to discover how to harness the power of resilience and cultivate a mindset of abundance and wealth.

Identifying Mindset and Strategies for Bouncing Back from Loss

Resilience often hinges on possessing a mindset that embraces setbacks as opportunities for growth and strength. When faced with adversity, it's essential to adopt a perspective that acknowledges the difficulty while simultaneously seeking out the potential for learning and development. Instead of dwelling on the pain or disappointment of loss, focus on the valuable lessons it can impart. **Shift your mindset toward finding the silver lining, extracting wisdom from the experience, and using it as a catalyst for personal growth.**

Strategies for bouncing back from loss start with acknowledging your emotions and allowing yourself to process them fully. **Instead of suppressing or ignoring feelings of grief, take the time to experience and understand them. This allows for a more complete healing process, enabling you to move forward with a clearer perspective.** Once you've acknowledged your emotions, it's crucial to reframe your thoughts. Challenge negative beliefs and replace them with affirming, empowering ones. **Focus on the potential for new beginnings and positive outcomes, steering your thoughts toward resilience and optimism.**

Practical strategies for bouncing back involve setting clear, achievable goals. **Establishing realistic milestones and measurable targets provides a roadmap for progress and growth.** Break down your goals into actionable steps, each one leading you closer to reclaiming stability and prosperity. Cultivate a mindset of persistence and tenacity, unwavering in your commitment to overcoming obstacles. **Embrace a proactive approach that acknowledges setbacks as temporary roadblocks rather than insurmountable barriers.**

Leverage your support system to bolster your resilience. **Surround yourself with individuals who uplift and encourage you, offering guidance and companionship. Seek out mentors or role models who have overcome similar challenges and draw strength from their experiences.** Additionally, prioritize self-care practices that nourish your physical, emotional, and mental well-being. **By addressing your needs and nurturing yourself, you fortify your ability to rebound from adversity.**

Bouncing back from loss often involves cultivating a mindset of gratitude and abundance. **Focusing on the blessings in your life and appreciating the resources at your disposal shifts your perspective to one of abundance rather than scarcity. This mindset positions you to attract opportunities and prosperity into your life.** Embrace the power of affirmations and visualization, harnessing the creative force of your thoughts to manifest your desires. **Envision the future you desire and affirm your ability to achieve it, thereby programming your mind for success.**

In implementing these strategies, remember the importance of self-compassion and patience. **Progress in the aftermath of loss may not occur at a linear pace, and setbacks are to be expected. Treat yourself with kindness and understanding as you navigate the journey toward resilience and prosperity. Celebrate every small victory, recognizing the strength and resilience within you.** By cultivating a positive mindset and implementing actionable strategies, you position yourself to bounce back from loss, empowered to reclaim joy and prosperity.

A Framework for Wealthy Living

Cultivating an abundance and wealth mindset isn't just about wishing for more; it's about creating systemic change in your approach to life. To assist in this transformative journey, let's introduce a practical framework: the **RICHES Model**. This acronym stands for Reflection, Intention, Commitment, Habituation, Evaluation, and Sustenance. Each stage is designed to guide you from understanding your current position to achieving a sustainable and prosperous state of mind and life.

Reflection: Self-Discovery as the Foundation

Wealth starts with **understanding who you are**, including your values, beliefs, and what you genuinely want in life. Reflection involves an honest assessment of these areas and acknowledgement of strengths and weaknesses. Begin by asking yourself deep, penetrating questions about what truly matters to you. What brings you joy? What are you passionate about? These answers provide the compass for your journey toward abundance.

Intention: Clear Goal Setting with Purpose

Once you've reflected on your values and passions, it's time to set your intentions. **Goals should emanate from your reflections** and be both ambitious and attainable. Align your financial and personal aspirations with your core values; this congruence is what powers a truly abundant mindset. Be explicit about what you wish to achieve and by when, crafting a vision for your life that excites and motivates you.

Commitment: Establishing Your Path to Achievement

Commitment translates intentions into plans. It requires dedicated thought about the **steps necessary to reach your goals**. This phase necessitates resource assessment, pinpointing what you'll need in terms of time, finances, and support. Establish a clear timeline and build in checkpoints for accountability along the way. Your level of commitment often determines your level of success.

Habituation: Consistent Actions Yield Results

Once committed, you must cultivate consistent behaviors that support your goals. **Successful wealth creation is the product of daily habits**, not one-off events. Integrate activities into your routine that bring you closer to your financial targets. Build systems and structures in your life that make these new habits almost second nature, ensuring you can maintain them even when motivation wanes.

Evaluation: Assessing and Adapting

Periodic evaluation is crucial in the journey towards a mindset of abundance and wealth. **Measure your progress, celebrate your wins**, and learn from any setbacks. By evaluating, you can make informed decisions about what to continue, what to improve, and what to abandon. This feedback loop is essential for growth and resilience, ensuring you stay agile and responsive to change.

Sustenance: Maintaining Momentum

The final step in the RICHES model is about maintaining the momentum built through your efforts. **Sustenance is about scaling your actions** to keep prospering and ensuring continuous growth. It's about broadening your knowledge, investing in relationships, and giving back, all of which serve to reinforce your abundance mindset. An essential part of this is self-care, which ensures you have the energy and health to enjoy the wealth you've created.

By following the RICHES model, you create a solid blueprint for cultivating an abundance and wealth mindset rooted in self-understanding and informed by thoughtful planning and persistent action. Remember that each step is iterative, as your goals and circumstances will evolve over time. This framework isn't just a linear path but a cyclical process that adapts with you, fostering continual success and prosperity.

The beauty of this model lies not just in its structured approach, but also in the mindset shifts that occur as you progress. As you grow richer in resources, relationships, and personal wellbeing, you'll find that the pursuit of wealth is about more than just material gain—it's about creating a life enriched with purpose and joy.

In times of loss and setback, it is crucial to understand the resilience and potential for prosperity that lies within us. Our mindset and strategies for bouncing back from adversity play a pivotal role in shaping our future. By cultivating a mindset of abundance and wealth, we can activate our God-given superpowers to create a happy, healthy, whole, and rich life.

Understanding Resilience: Recognizing that setbacks are not permanent roadblocks but rather temporary detours empowers us to tap into our resilience. Every setback holds within it the seeds of opportunity for growth and transformation. It's essential to view challenges as stepping stones toward greater success, thereby allowing us to bounce back with renewed vigor.

Mindset for Bouncing Back: Cultivating a growth mindset is a crucial step in bouncing back from loss. Embracing the belief that challenges are opportunities for learning and development rather than insurmountable obstacles allows us to approach setbacks with a sense of optimism and flexibility. By reframing our perspective, we can harness the power to overcome adversity and thrive in the face of challenges.

Strategies for Prosperity: Adopting proactive strategies such as setting clear goals, developing a strong support network, and building resilience through self-care practices are key to harnessing resilience and promoting prosperity after loss. By focusing on what we can control, taking consistent action, and persistently pursuing our aspirations, we can shift our trajectory toward a future filled with abundance and success.

As we integrate these insights and strategies into our lives, we begin to transform our reality. By unlocking our innate capacity for resilience and cultivating a mindset of abundance and wealth, we can stride confidently toward a fulfilling, prosperous, and empowered life. The journey to bounce back from loss is not only about overcoming adversity but also about emerging even stronger and more prosperous than before, ready to unleash the full extent of our God-given superpowers to manifest a life of limitless potential.

Chapter 10: Releasing Envy and Resentment for Prosperity

"They will never be YOU. And that is the true gift."

The afternoon light streamed in through the tall windows of a cozy study room, bathing the space in a warm golden hue. Amidst shelves heavy with books and a desk cluttered with the detritus of academic toil, a woman stared at the pages of a journal, so intently as if to will the ink to rearrange itself into clearer answers. Emma, a psychology graduate student, was grappling with the invisible threads that wound through her relationships: strands of envy and resentment she had begun to acknowledge but could not yet unravel.

She breathed in the musty scent of aging paper, a comforting backdrop to the turmoil of self-reflection. Emma recalled a conversation with her mentor when he said, "To find fulfillment, Emma, you must navigate the labyrinth of the soul and confront the monsters within." It was an allegory for personal growth, challenging her to face the habits that she knew deep down were holding her back.

A gust of wind rattled the windowpane, drawing her attention away from the gnawing thoughts. The sound mingled with the distant laughter of fellow students outside, a stark contrast to the silent battle raging within her. She imagined the envy rooted within her like weeds in a garden, sucking vitality from the soil, robbing her potential to flourish.

The sound of keys in the door interrupted her train of thought. Her roommate, a shining example of serenity, entered the room with a quiet grace. Emma often wondered how someone could be so at peace amidst the chaos of graduate studies. Was it her roommate's lack of envy, her acceptance of life's imperfections? Emma's desire to emulate that tranquility sparked a pang of jealousy, an irony not lost on her as she pondered their contrasting emotional landscapes.

She rose from her seat, the movement a physical attempt to shake the paralysis that threatened to take root alongside her negative emotions. The late afternoon light caught the edges of her vision, bathing the room in a soft glow that seemed to hold a promise: the possibility of transformation if she could only step through the shadows of her own making.

Emma made a silent vow to herself as she closed the journal and turned to her roommate with a smile that was a trifle more genuine than it had been in weeks. She would start small, removing one stone of resentment at a time to clear the path towards abundance and personal fulfillment. As the day waned and the weight of her resolve settled in her chest, Emma wondered, how does one quantify success on such a deeply personal journey?

Dare to Let Go and Flourish

When the mind clings to envy and resentment like a ship anchored in stormy waters, the prospect of steering towards the shores of prosperity seems nothing short of a herculean endeavor. Yet, herein lies the cornerstone of transformation. You stand at the brink of reclaiming your power, which until now, has been leashed by the very emotions that intend to protect, yet paradoxically imprison. This journey is about identifying the invisible chains of envy and resentment that restrict you so that you can sever them and be free to prosper.

Understanding the Undercurrents of Envy and Resentment is a pivotal step. These emotions often operate covertly, entrenched in the back alleys of our subconscious, shaping our beliefs and actions without a whisper of their existence. The acknowledgment of their presence is the beacon that will guide you to brighter landscapes of the spirit. As we shine a light on these hidden patterns, we realize that what we believed to be part of our fundamental nature is, in fact, an imposed narrative—a collective conditioning that does not serve our highest self.

Confronting and releasing these habits is as vital to our growth as the air we breathe. To do so, we must first become conscious of the stories we tell ourselves, the justifications we invent for holding onto pain. This emotional alchemy—transmuting the leaden weight of resentment into the gold of wisdom—is the catalyst for a life of abundance. It is not just a process of thought but also of action. **Clearing Paths for Abundance** means to actively engage with these emotions, to negotiate peace with them, and in turn, permit ourselves to access a future brimming with fulfillment.

Throughout this book, we have explored the activation of your God-given superpowers to construct a reality both fulfilling and rich. As you turn each page, you have unraveled your conditioned belief systems and have been learning how to foster an existence that resonates with vibrancy and authenticity. Before you now stands the final but perhaps the most transformative principle: the detachment from the emotional restraints of envy and resentment. It is here where the totality of this book's wisdom culminates into the ultimate leap toward a liberated life.

The Great Unshackling: A Step-by-Step Escape Plan

1. Identify societal conditioning: Reflect deeply on your life scripts and how societal norms have invisibly shaped them. Write down these influences and acknowledge that they once held sway over your perceptions and decisions.

2. Question societal conditioning: Challenge the roots of your long-held beliefs. Ask yourself critical questions—do these conditioned responses truly represent who I am, and do they contribute to my welfare?

3. Define your own values: It is time to redefine your moral compass. What truly ignites your passion and fulfillment? Jot down your fundamental values and let this manifesto guide your future choices.

4. Surround yourself with like-minded individuals: Cultivate a garden of relationships that resonates with your authentic self. Seek out communities where your newly defined values are supported and where you can flourish.

5. Practice self-expression: Find your voice in the symphony of life. Experiment with various forms of self-expression that feel right for you, from art to activism, and let the world hear your song, unfettered by the whispers of judgment.

6. Set boundaries: Be the guardian of your territory of peace. Learn to decline what does not align with your core values, and safeguard your time, energy, and emotional space.

As each step is taken, keep in mind your right and ability to adjust the sails—but always keep your destination in sight. Continuously evaluate your progress, gauging the improvement of your emotional well-being as much as the tangibility of your prosperity.

Set a time frame for these actions, perhaps over a month, to instill a sense of urgency and commitment. At the end of this structured time, look back and you will see not the person who was held back by silent resentments and envies but one who stands tall and free, ready to grasp a life of untold abundance.

Allow this journey to be your testimony that strength is not in the continuation of the battle but in the bravery of letting go. As you walk this path, remember that your potential is limitless and that prosperity—of mind, body, and soul—is not simply a goal but a natural state of a liberated spirit. Trust that by embracing these practices, you are not just dreaming of a better future—you are constructing it with every conscious thought and action.

Are you aware of the subtle ways envy and resentment may be holding you back from prosperity? Identifying hidden patterns of envy and resentment is the first step to releasing their grip on your life. These negative emotions can often linger beneath the surface, affecting our thoughts, emotions, and actions without us even realizing it. Left unchecked, they can hinder personal growth and block the path to abundance and fulfillment.

Envy can arise when we compare ourselves to others, feeling a sense of lack or unfairness when we perceive someone else as having something we desire. It can create feelings of insecurity, bitterness, and discontentment, leading us to resent those who seem to have what we want. Resentment, on the other hand, stems from holding onto past hurts, disappointments, or perceived injustices. It can fester within us, poisoning our outlook on life and hindering our ability to move forward.

Identifying these hidden patterns of envy and resentment is crucial for personal growth and prosperity.

The first step in breaking free from these negative emotions is recognizing their presence in our lives. Take time to reflect on your thoughts and feelings when it comes to your experiences with others. Are there times when you feel a twinge of envy or a pang of resentment? Do you catch yourself comparing your life to others and feeling a sense of lack? Awareness is the key to unlocking these hidden patterns and taking the necessary steps to release them.

By confronting these patterns head-on, you can begin to dismantle their hold on your life.

It's important to understand that envy and resentment are natural human emotions. They are not signs of weakness or failure, but rather opportunities for growth and transformation. When we acknowledge their presence, we empower ourselves to address them with compassion and understanding. By shining a light on these hidden patterns, we can start to unravel their grip on our thoughts and emotions, creating space for new perspectives and positive change.

Ready to confront and release these habits that hinder personal growth? Keep reading and discover actionable steps to clear the path for abundance and fulfillment in your life.

Identifying hidden patterns of envy and resentment is crucial to our personal growth and overall well-being. But once we've recognized these negative emotions, we must confront and release the habits that have been hindering our progress. It's not enough to simply acknowledge the envy and resentment; we must take proactive steps to eliminate them from our lives.

One of the first steps in confronting these habits is to recognize when envy and resentment are arising within us. **Be mindful** of your feelings, thoughts, and reactions. When you find yourself experiencing envy or resentment, take a moment to pause and reflect on the underlying causes. **Ask yourself** why you are feeling this way and what triggers these emotions. Developing this awareness will allow you to address and ultimately release these destructive patterns.

Confronting harmful habits also involves taking responsibility for our emotions and actions. Instead of blaming external factors for our envy and resentment, we must acknowledge our own role in cultivating these negative sentiments. **By taking ownership**, we gain the power to change our responses and shift our perspective. This is a crucial step in breaking free from the grip of envy and resentment.

In order to release these detrimental habits, we must actively work towards cultivating a mindset of abundance and gratitude. **Practice gratitude daily** by acknowledging the blessings in your life, both big and small. This shift in focus from scarcity to abundance will help dismantle the roots of envy and resentment within you. **Cultivate an abundance mentality** by celebrating the success of others and recognizing that their achievements do not diminish your own potential for success.

Seek to understand the root cause of your envy and resentment. Dig deep to uncover the underlying insecurities, fears, or unmet desires that are fueling these emotions. **Confronting and addressing these root causes** will enable you to release the grip of envy and resentment and pave the way for personal growth and fulfillment.

Another vital step in releasing these habits is to surround yourself with positive influences. **Spend time with supportive and uplifting**

individuals who inspire and encourage you to be your best self. Limit exposure to negative environments and toxic relationships that fuel feelings of envy and resentment. **Choose to fill your life with positivity** and seek out mentors and role models who exemplify the qualities and mindset you aspire to cultivate.

In confronting and releasing habits that hinder personal growth, it's essential to remember that this is an ongoing process. **It requires consistent effort and self-reflection** to uproot deeply ingrained patterns. But by confronting these habits head-on and taking active steps to release them, we create space for abundance and fulfillment to flow into our lives. This journey of growth and transformation is a deliberate, ongoing practice that requires patience, determination, and a steadfast commitment to personal evolution.

Unlocking Emotional Shackles

When we speak of abundance and prosperity, it's essential to understand that they're not just about material wealth. They embody a **state of wellbeing** where every facet of your life flourishes. However, negative emotions like envy and resentment can be substantial blocks to this state—think of them as emotional shackles, holding you back from your full potential. Addressing these feelings is not just beneficial; it is **imperative** to pave a clear path toward a richer, more fulfilling existence.

Cultivating Emotional Intelligence

One of the most powerful tools at your disposal is the ability to cultivate emotional intelligence. This involves **recognizing**, **understanding**, and **managing** your emotions, turning potentially destructive feelings into constructive actions. Begin by observing your reactions in situations that typically trigger envy or resentment. Are there patterns in the people or events that ignite these feelings? By becoming aware of triggers, you take the first step toward regaining control over your emotional life.

The Power of Forgiveness

Forgiveness is one of your inner superhero's most profound powers. It's about releasing the burden for your own peace of mind, not necessarily condoning another's behavior. Forgiveness frees up mental space that was previously consumed by negative emotions. To practice forgiveness, reflect on the situation causing resentment, acknowledge your feelings, and actively decide to let go. This isn't a one-off event but a process that you might need to revisit to fully clear the emotional debris.

Affirm Your Worth

Envy often stems from a sense of inadequacy, while resentment can arise from a feeling of being wronged or undervalued. *Affirmations* can reinforce your self-worth and counter these negative emotions. Create **personal affirmations** that resonate with your aspirations and recite them daily. Remember, words possess power—speak them with conviction and belief to manifest the life you desire.

Change Your Narrative

How we interpret our circumstances can greatly influence our emotional state. Shifting your narrative from one of lack and limitation to one of appreciation and potential can have a profound impact on your emotional health. Rather than focusing on what others have, redirect your attention to gratitude for what you already possess and for the opportunities that lie ahead. This altered perspective is a cornerstone of a prosperous life.

Transformative Actions

Transcending negative emotions isn't just about changing how you feel; it's about converting those feelings into **transformative actions**. Use the energy from your emotions as fuel to drive you towards new learning experiences, altered career paths, or improved relationships. These actions will not only distract you from destructive feelings but also build a foundation for personal growth and success.

Consistent Self-Care

Never underestimate the power of self-care in maintaining a healthy emotional balance. It might seem simple, but actions such as ensuring adequate sleep, eating well, exercising, and taking time for leisure activities are fundamental in managing stress and preventing the buildup of envy and resentment. Caring for yourself sends a message to your subconscious that **you are valuable**, bolstering resilience to negative emotions.

Anchoring In The Present

Lastly, practice being present in the moment. When your mind sways towards envy or resentment, gently bring your focus back to the here and now. By being mindful, you can appreciate the fullness of each experience, reduce the power of past grievances, and lessen the sting of comparison that future-oriented envy can bring. In the present, you will find a powerful ally in the pursuit of abundance and fulfillment.

Remember, releasing envy and resentment is a **dynamic process** that requires ongoing attention and commitment. However, by continually engaging in these practices, you will free yourself to embrace a life of prosperity that surpasses mere monetary wealth, one brimming with joy, peace, and gratification.

In your journey to releasing envy and resentment for prosperity, you've uncovered hidden patterns of negativity that have been holding you back. By identifying these destructive patterns in your life, you've taken the crucial first step toward true personal growth and abundance.

Now armed with the awareness of these hidden patterns, you're ready to confront and release the habits that hinder your progress. By acknowledging the negative emotions of envy and resentment, you've cleared a path for abundance and fulfillment. You've made a powerful decision to reclaim your inner peace and create a space for prosperity in your life.

It's essential to remember that releasing envy and resentment isn't just about letting go of negative emotions; it's about making space

for positive energy in your life. As you release these destructive patterns, you pave the way for happiness, health, wholeness, and richness. You've learned that true prosperity isn't just about financial wealth, but about a life filled with joy, purpose, and fulfillment.

This journey has revealed the profound impact of addressing negative emotions on your overall well-being and success. By addressing and releasing envy and resentment, you've empowered yourself to step into your God-given superpowers, and you're now equipped to create a life of abundance and prosperity on your own terms.

Remember, this journey doesn't end here. It's an ongoing process of self-discovery, growth, and empowerment. As you move forward, continue to cultivate the positive energy you've created and nurture the abundance you've welcomed into your life. Embrace your newfound freedom from envy and resentment, and watch as prosperity flows into every area of your life.

Congratulations on completing this transformative chapter. You've taken a giant leap toward living a happy, healthy, whole, and rich life. Now, go forth and unleash your inner superhero to create the life you deserve.

Unleashing Your Inner Superhero: The Journey Forward

As we draw the curtain on this transformative journey, it's time to look back and marvel at the ground we've covered together. This book has not just been about reading; it's been about evolving, challenging deep-seated beliefs, and stepping into the power that has always been within you. Now, equipped with the knowledge and tools to transcend your limitations, you stand at the threshold of a life redefined by happiness, health, wholeness, and wealth.

Real-world applications of the teachings in this book are endless and as unique as you are. Whether you're a professional aiming for the next level in your career, an entrepreneur seeking to scale your business, or an individual striving for personal growth, the principles shared here are your roadmap. Implement these strategies with unwavering consistency, and watch as the world around you begins to transform.

Let's briefly **recap the main ideas**: We explored the significance of understanding our inherent superpowers – those unique gifts and abilities given to us by a higher power. We delved into strategies for unwinding the ingrained beliefs that limit our potential, emphasizing the importance of a mindset shift towards abundance and possibility. Importantly, we discussed the practical steps needed to manifest a life filled with joy, fulfillment, and prosperity.

Putting these insights into action means starting with small, daily changes. Reflect on your routines, the words you speak to yourself, and the thoughts that occupy your mind. Challenge yourself to replace any negativity with positivity and gratitude. Set clear, actionable goals and review them regularly to track your progress. Remember, the path to a fulfilled life is both a sprint and a marathon – immediate actions lead to long-term transformations.

It is with humility that I acknowledge the **limitations of this work**.

While comprehensive, there are realms of personal growth and development that require continuous exploration. I encourage you to view this book not as an endpoint but as a milestone in your lifelong journey of learning and self-discovery.

You are empowered to take action, to make changes, and to shape your destiny. Let the insights gleaned from these pages fuel your courage to break free from what holds you back. Embrace your inner superhero, and let your light shine forth, illuminating the path for others as you go.

As we part ways, I leave you with **a memorable and impactful thought**: You possess an infinite reservoir of potential, and the key to unleashing it lies within you. Dive deep, explore fearlessly, and let nothing dim the brilliance of your light.

"Our deepest fear is not that we are inadequate. Our deepest fear is that we are powerful beyond measure. It is our light, not our darkness, that most frightens us." - Marianne Williamson

Go forth, equipped with the knowledge that you are more powerful than you have ever imagined. The world awaits the wonders you are about to unleash.

Resources

If you want a safe place to explore these concepts so you can develop a happy, healthy, whole and rich life, join the GLOW program. It is $47 per month. Because you purchased this book, you can try it out for $1.

https://www.happyhealthywholerich.com/offers/zJLoAGy4

Want me to coach you to a happier, healthier, whole and richer lifestyle? Join Club Level Access. This coaching program will help you start from exactly where you are and activate your superpowers within. You deserve the life of your dreams https://www.happyhealthywholerich.com/offers/EmbK9oBz

Looking for like minded women who are changing the world? Join the Happy, Healthy, Whole & Rich Mastermind. Contact support@tinabrinkleypotts for more information

Leave a Review:

Thank you for embarking on this transformative journey with me through the pages of "God-Powered: Unleashing Your Inner Superhero for a Happy, Healthy, Whole, and Rich Life." I hope that you found inspiration, insights, and practical tools to help you unleash your inner superhero and live a life of purpose, abundance, and fulfillment.

Your feedback is invaluable in helping others discover this empowering message. If you found this book helpful, I would greatly appreciate it if you could take a moment to leave a review on Amazon or Goodreads. Your review will not only support the continued success of this book but also guide fellow seekers on their own journeys of self-discovery and empowerment.

Thank you for being a part of this community of superheroes. Together, we can create a ripple effect of positive change in the world. Keep shining your light brightly, and may your journey be filled with boundless joy and blessings.

Other Books by Tina Brinkley Potts

Automated Business Empire: Build A Massive Community And Scale Your Business With Heart-Centered Marketing

The Heart of the Machine: Cultivating Your Business Garden in the Digital Age

Feel the Pulse of Your Growing Empire

Does the thought of marketing automation send chills down your spine, conjuring visions of cold, impersonal customer interactions? Yet, do you yearn for the expanse of your business to stretch far and wide? Rest easy, dear friend, for the path you seek is at your fingertips, warmly guiding you through the marriage of efficiency and soul.

A Curious Fact, A Pivotal Question

Have you ever pondered the paradox that as our digital capabilities skyrocket, our connections can become superficial? This doesn't have to be your reality. Transform this challenge into your strength; let's delve into the art of nurturing your garden of customers with the finesse of a gardener and the precision of a master clockmaker.

Embrace the Connection

Envision your business not merely as a purveyor of goods or services but as a flourishing community, vibrant and alive with connection. Each client interaction is a seed of trust, and with the wisdom contained in these pages, you can cultivate a thriving ecosystem that blooms with loyalty and engagement.

The Companion to Your Entrepreneurial Journey

Unveiling the Blueprint to Your Business's Heartbeat

"Nurturing Automation" is more than a guide—it's the compass that aligns the mechanical gears of automation with the human touch of your heartbeat. Step into a world where your business grows effortlessly, and each customer feels the warmth of your personal care pulsating through every interaction.

Core Pillars of Heart-Centered Expansion

Synchronized Steps: Blending Efficiency with Compassion

The Pulse of Personalization: Behavior-Based Marketing Mastery

Emotional Alchemy in Automation: Stirring the Soul in Systems

Crafting a Client Odyssey: The Art of Tech-Tendered Tales

Fostering Lasting Bonds: Strategies for Continual Customer Cultivation

The Gentle Art of Upsells and Downsells: Dance of the Insightful Entrepreneur

Audience Behavior Deciphering: The Heartbeat Metrics

The Charisma Factor: Personality as Magnetic Polarity in Marketing

Orchestrating a Symphony of Connections: Streamlined Nurturing Systems

Thriving Roots: Empowerment Through Strategic Gardening Skills

The Visionaries Who Will Cultivate Empires

Are you the spirited business owner with a vision larger than life but a heart fiercely protective of every individual relationship? Do you lie awake wondering how to keep the personalized touch in a rapidly automating world? This book was crafted with your dreams and concerns in hand, eagerly waiting to help you transition into the grand next stage of your business legacy.

Reap the Harvest: What Blooms from These Pages

Nurture the growth of your enterprise with the secrets nestled within this tome. You'll emerge not just with a system but a manifesto for a revolution in how we think about business growth in harmony with customer care.

Distinctive Advantages of this Heartfelt Approach

Harmonizing automation with the human spirit

Building a framework for lasting customer relationships

Personalized marketing strategies that resonate

Embracing emotions as a powerful marketing tool

A narrative customer journey that's both efficient and genuine

Fostering authentic connections for continuing engagement

Cultivating insight through customer behavior analysis

Amplifying your unique voice in a world of echoes

Engineering a nurturing network that cradles your brand's expansion

Gearing up for growth with a foundation of sincere leadership

Lessons with Immediate Life

Enlighten your marketing with wisdom steeped in experience and empathy. Implement the strategies herein with confidence, encouraging each customer to grow alongside you. Learn how to whisper through wires, ensuring your digital footprint is as warm and inviting as your handshake.

From a Spark to an Eternal Flame: Your Journey Awaits

Ignite Your Path Now

Are you prepared to discover the rhythm that guides a flourishing community? To carve out a niche where every digital footprint glows with purpose and passion? Lay claim to your copy of "Nurturing Automation: Build a Massive Community and Scale Your Business with Heart-Centered Marketing" and step into the role of the luminary entrepreneur you were meant to be.

Your Hand on the Plow, Eyes on the Horizon

This is not merely a transaction; it is an investment in your legacy, a pledge to the soul of your enterprise. Arm yourself with the knowledge to tenderly sculpt a space where every customer feels cherished while your reach extends further than you dared to dream. With a deep breath and courageous heart, embark on this transformative odyssey now.

The wisdom you'll encounter in this book is woven with relatable anecdotes and compassionate guidance, speaking directly to the heart of the savvy business owner yearning for connection in an automated world. We speak on terms of understanding, solidarity, and shared aspirations.

Through colorful metaphors and sensory language, we'll uncover how each chapter of this book is a stepping stone across the river of progress, leaving you invigorated and prepared to embrace a nurturing approach that is genuinely scalable.

Once you've turned the final page, you'll stand upon the shore of newfound knowledge, ready to apply these time-tested principles and eager to see where they will lead your enterprise and its cherished patrons.

Welcome the dawn of your business's brightest chapter. Allow "Nurturing Automation" to be the compass that guides your entrepreneurial ship through the digital tides. Claim your passage, and let's set sail to horizons of heart-centered triumph!

KnowNet Worth: Unearthing Your Intellectual Wealth

Are you struggling to monetize your intellectual property and establish yourself as a thought leader in a crowded marketplace?

Do you dream of amplifying your voice, crafting your authority, and striking it rich in the knowledge economy?

Imagine finally breaking through the noise, standing out as a respected expert, and creating multiple income streams from your unique expertise.

KnowNet Worth is a comprehensive guide designed to help individuals like you unleash their intellectual wealth, cultivate their authority, and thrive in the

competitive world of thought leadership.

Crafting the 'IT' Factor in Thought Leadership

Diversifying Your Knowledge Assets

Mastering Customer Journey Automation

Target audience

Professionals, consultants, and entrepreneurs looking to elevate their thought leadership game, create impactful content, and automate systems for scalable business growth.

By the end of this book, you will have mastered the art of developing and marketing your unique offerings, diversifying your income streams, and automating customer journeys for sustained business growth.

Ready to unlock your intellectual wealth, craft your authority, and strike it rich in the knowledge economy? Get your copy of KnowNet Worth now!

www.ingramcontent.com/pod-product-compliance
Lightning Source LLC
Chambersburg PA
CBHW030439010526
44118CB00011B/714